BRITISH MUSEUM PATTERN BOOKS

Pacific Designs

Pacific Designs

REBECCA JEWELL

Introduction by Jude Lloyd

British Museum Press

First published in 1998 by
British Museum Press
A division of The British
Museum Company Ltd
46 Bloomsbury Street
London WC1B 3QQ

A catalogue record for this
book is available from the
British Library
ISBN 0–7141–8076–9

Design by Roger Davies
Typeset in Palatino by
Wyvern 21 Ltd, Bristol
Printed in Great Britain by
Page Bros, Norwich

Acknowledgements
We would like to thank Dr John
Mack, Keeper of the Department
of Ethnography in the British
Museum, for allowing access to
the enormous collections of
Pacific material. We are grateful
also to the many members of
staff in the Department and its
Students' Room, particularly
Michael O'Hanlon, for their
advice and comments on this
book. Thanks also to Jill Hasell
for her help, patience and advice
while Rebecca sifted through the
collections in the stores. Finally,
we would like to thank our
families – Jake, Agnes, Theo,
Dora, William, Hugh and
Anne – for giving us their time
and support in the production
of this book.

Contents

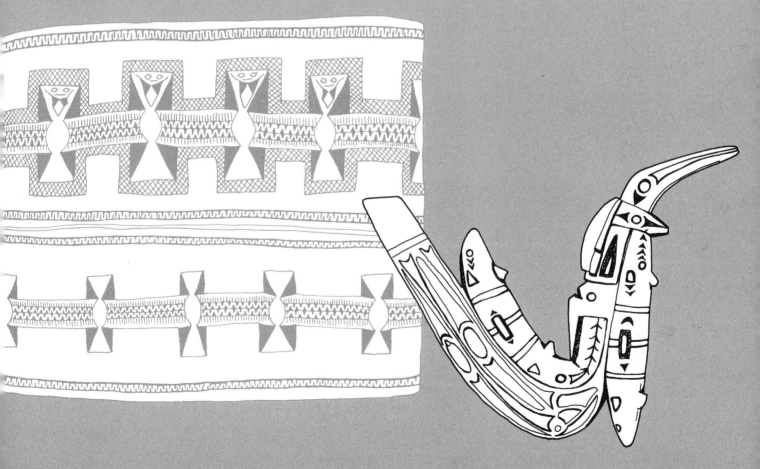

CHINA

TAIWAN

HONG KONG

PHILIPPINES

MALAYSIA

BORNEO

INDONESIA

IRIAN JAYA

BELAU

CAROLINE ISLANDS

MICRONESIA

NORTH PACIFIC

MARSHALL
ISLANDS

POHNPEI

GILBERT
ISLANDS

NAURU

KIRIBATI

MELANESIA

TUVALU

BOUGAINVILLE

SOLOMON
ISLANDS

MALAITA

SANTA
ISABEL

SANTA
CRUZ
ISLANDS

BANKS
ISLANDS

VANUATU

WEST
SA

WALLIS
AND
FUTUNA

FIJI ISLANDS

NEW CALEDONIA

T

1 2
PAPUA
4 3 Madang
5
8
Port Moresby

12

11

7 6

10
9

TORRES STRAIT
ISLANDS

NEW

GUINEA

Darwin
RAMINGINING
ARNHEMLAND

THE
Broome KIMBERLEYS

COSSACK
HAMMERSLEY
RANGE

WESTERN AUSTRALIA

Perth

NORTHERN
TERRITORY

AUSTRALIA

SOUTH AUSTRALIA

Adelaide

VICTORIA
Melbourne

Cairns

QUEENSLAND

Brisbane

NEW SOUTH WALES

Sydney
Canberra

NORTH ISLAND
Auckland

Wellington

NEW ZEALAND

Hobart

SOUTH ISLAND

INDIAN OCEAN

MEXICO

OCEAN

ISLANDS

Honolulu ◦ HAWAII

GALAPAGOS
ISLANDS

MARQUESAS ISLANDS

FATU-HIVA

FRENCH POLYNESIA

ICAN
OA

SOCIETY
ISLANDS

COOK
ISLANDS

MANGAI

AUSTRAL ISLANDS

TAHITI

MANUAE

RAROTONGA

PITCAIRN ISLANDS

GROUP

POLYNESIA

EASTER ISLAND

SOUTH   PACIFIC

OCEAN

PAPUA NEW GUINEA

1 HERMIT ISLAND
2 MANUS ISLAND
3 EAST SEPIK
4 WEST SEPIK
5 MOUNT HAGEN
6 TAMI ISLAND
7 HUON GULF
8 GULF OF PAPUA
9 MILNE BAY
10 TROBRIAND ISLANDS
11 NEW BRITAIN
12 NEW IRELAND

500   1000 km

200   400   600 miles

Preface

The drawings in this book are taken from objects in the collections of the Ethnography Department of the British Museum. The designs are grouped by geography and ethnography, as they are in the Museum's collections, although national borders may not now be the same as these ethnographic boundaries. For example, Irian Jaya is today part of Indonesia, but artefacts from the region are stored with the Melanesian collections. Fiji is ethnographically similar to its neighbouring Polynesian Islands, although it is often considered part of Melanesia. Artefacts from Bougainville are grouped with those from the Solomon Islands, despite the fact that politically it is a province of Papua New Guinea. Modern place names are used throughout the book for localities of the objects.

I have tried to include designs from as many islands as possible to give a sense of the range of material and diversity of artistic expression in the Pacific. Objects have been chosen for people interested in design, and I wanted to reproduce a representative range of images, patterns, shapes and textures. These are found on or incorporated within a variety of media including stone, turtle-shell, pottery, wood, bamboo, gourds, basketware, coconut shells, barkcloth, bone, feathers and sea shells. Some of the Museum's collections, however, like those from the Pitcairn Islands, contain no ornate or decorative pieces suitable for inclusion in this book. Another restriction was the suitability of the objects to be represented clearly in black and white line drawings, and for this reason many objects and art works in the collections, such as Australian Aboriginal dot paintings, are not included. I have also tried to isolate patterns and to simplify them, an inevitable necessity of moving from three dimensions to two; the illustrations of the Cook Islands adzes (**23**) are one example. On other occasions, when the shapes of the objects are in themselves interesting, such as the Tami headrests (**61**), I have included the whole artefact.

Background information on some of the objects and about the peoples who made them can be found in the Introduction and in the captions. More detail on individual pieces, such as indigenous names for objects (where known), their functions or method of manufacture, as well as their museum registration numbers, is included in the Notes.

My aim has been to provide a pictorial record of just some of the beautifully decorated and crafted objects in the Pacific collections of the British Museum. As with the other books in this Pattern Book series, I hope *Pacific Designs* will provide source material for practising artists, potters, textile designers, teachers and others interested in the history of Pacific art and culture.

REBECCA JEWELL

Introduction

The vast Pacific Ocean is populated with many seaboard and mainland peoples dependent on the ocean as a source not only of food but also of tools and trading objects. Trade in any culture has much greater significance than the simple exchange of goods – it is also an opportunity to gain kudos among one's own people (by being seen to trade well), to forge alliances with others, to make matches – indeed, to contribute to the survival of one's whole way of life. Given the importance of trade in such a diverse area as that of the Pacific, it is not surprising that skills of navigation and canoe-building flourished (49). Early European visitors were stunned to see ocean-going canoes of up to 20 m in length, capable of long-distance travel and commerce. Shipboard calculation of longitude was a novelty in the late eighteenth century, and Europeans were amazed by the journeys of which seemingly primitive people appeared capable.

Pacific island culture has long fascinated the Western world, and not solely from an academic or scientific point of view. As early as 1785, the Pacific arena entered popular culture in the form of a pantomime depicting the apotheosis of Captain Cook, and it has been the subject of popular film and literature ever since. Despite the vastness of the Pacific there appeared to be a homogeneity of culture, certainly in Polynesia, which led to questions about how pre-literate peoples could have developed such skill in long-distance navigation. In this century, reconstructions such as Thor Heyerdahl's *Kon-Tiki* voyages demonstrate the undying fascination with the spread of broadly common Pacific cultures.

Social scientists have traditionally divided the Pacific area into four regions: Australia, including the Australian continent and inshore islands; Melanesia, referring to the island of New Guinea and the south-western islands as far as Fiji; Polynesia, including the central Pacific islands from Hawaii in the north to New Zealand in the south; and Micronesia, covering the islands to the east and north of the Philippines. Polynesia has sometimes been more generally called the South Seas. The four regions are also referred to collectively as Oceania.

While cultural similarities exist across enormous distances in the Pacific, it should also be noted that great diversity exists within each region, even between one village and the next. The origins of the populations of the Pacific region are the subject of much discussion. Suggestions have included South America, North America and South-east Asia, the last of which is the current consensus. Australia has the oldest continuous culture, estimated at 40,000 to 60,000 years, and archaeologists calculate New Guinea highland cultures to be approximately 30,000 years old. Research suggests that these are the oldest cultures in the region; Polynesian cultures are thought to be much younger, as recent as 4000 BC.

History

Words from Oceania such as *taboo*, *boomerang* and *tattoo* have become part of the English language, one indication of the impact of these cultures upon our own. Another is the influence on artists, including Gauguin and Picasso. However, the first works brought from Oceania to Europe were considered curiosities rather than art. Broadly speaking, Westerners were involved in the exploration and later colonisation of the Pacific as either scientists, adventurers, administrators or missionaries, and to the larger islands they also came as settlers. Collections such as those of the British Museum reflect the varied contacts these outsiders had with Pacific peoples, as well as the extent of their understanding of indigenous ways of life.

One of the first collections of artefacts from the South Seas to be exhibited publicly in Europe was acquired by the British Museum from Captain James Cook's voyages in the *Endeavour* and *Resolution*. A Tahitian stone pestle (**26**) is one example. The collection was displayed in the Otaheiti Room and included feathered cloaks from Hawaii, kava bowls, weaponry and so-called 'idols'. One such figure was found concealed within a mourning costume originally exhibited in the late 1700s; possibly placed there by islanders in order to safeguard the costume on its original journey, it was only discovered late in the twentieth century during conservation. Accounts of the voyages of discovery as well as the public and private exhibition of material culture, flora and fauna from the Pacific influenced many intellectuals, including Charles Darwin.

Some of the practices of Pacific societies as reported in popular books and scientific works, particularly ritualised cannibalism, head-hunting and the seeming absence of clothing, were abhorrent to the European sense of morality, and missionaries were quick to follow in the wake of the early explorers. The first missionaries to Tahiti, the Marquesas Islands and the Tongan Islands arrived in 1797/8, and soon other missionary posts were set up on more remote islands across the Pacific. Missionaries often brought objects back to Europe, sometimes bought or traded, occasionally stolen or taken away in the name of salvation, sometimes gifts from their Pacific hosts. Objects like the 'fisherman's god' from Rarotonga (**22**) might have been exhibited as signs of pagan savagery, historic reminders of nearly extinct cultures, or even for their artistic beauty. Objects were sold at public auction as a way of raising funds for those in the field, not all of whom were necessarily Europeans. After their 'success' in Fiji, Lifu, Niue and other Polynesian islands, the London Missionary Society (a large Protestant group) sponsored islanders from these regions to go to other areas of Oceania, on the assumption that they would not only be more easily received but better able to cope with tropical conditions than Europeans. The influence of these Polynesian missionary families can be seen in artistic styles, particularly barkcloth and weaving which, unlike masks and decorated skulls, were not considered pagan (**21**).

European influence was not limited to explorers and missionaries: traders, settlers, adventurers and sugar-planters were also discovering the commercial possibilities of the Pacific. In the late 1800s and early 1900s the newly explored regions of Melanesia became increasingly popular, and many Polynesian islanders were induced to set sail by the promise of great fortune. Although the days of slavery had formally ended, white masters still used dubious methods of coercion when recruiting local sugar-cane cutters, boat crews and *beche-de-mer* and pearl-shell divers. The traders' disruptive and sometimes immoral treatment of the islanders, coupled with the spread of European illnesses such as smallpox, venereal diseases and influenza, finally forced the British Government to take some responsibility for the islands, a century after taking possession of them –

no doubt influenced by the fact that the German, Dutch and French governments had also staked claims in the area. The island of New Guinea, for instance, was divided among Dutch (Irian Jaya), German (New Guinea) and British/Australian interests (Papua).

While artefacts from the distant South Seas had found their way to Britain in the early eighteenth century, it was not until the mid-nineteenth century that attempts were made to understand what these objects meant to the people who had made them. The discipline of anthropology was born from pioneering work such as A. C. Haddon's anthropological expeditions from Britain to Melanesia (1888 and 1898) and Franz Boas' expeditions from the United States to Canada (1886 and 1894). Both used material culture as a basis for understanding people and their way of life. Early anthropologists often brought back objects as representations of the societies they had visited and lived among (48, 62). Governors and administrators also contributed to the wealth of material being amassed in Britain and other nations. The study of such collections in the British Museum became, for some, less a study of the Pacific and more a historical document of an increasingly fragmenting society. Many believed that not only the cultures of Oceanic peoples but the peoples themselves were in danger of dying out.

Pacific peoples, however, responded to new ideas and technologies in innovative ways, negotiating with new trading partners and producing items adapted to European tastes to cater for the new markets. The Maori treasure boxes (6) – often deemed 'fakes' or 'forgeries' by British academics of the time – are an example. Iron tools were used to great effect by islanders, often resulting in flamboyant styles, and some of the earliest trade items were iron axes and smaller pieces of metal. In this century, acrylic painted canvases derived from Aboriginal Australian painting and sand drawings have acquired great popularity on the international art market (46, 47). Lithography and other types of printing have become a popular medium for Papua New Guinean artists. Another example of innovation is the use of Asian-produced cotton material called *calico* or *lava-lava*, once a popular trade item used by Europeans, which has become the national dress for many of the newly independent Pacific nations. Printed T-shirts are also a popular medium across Oceania for local designs and for sale to foreigners.

The British Museum collections reflect some of the extensive changes in Pacific island society in the late nineteenth and twentieth centuries as new religions, technologies and laws were vigorously imposed and sometimes willingly explored and adopted.

Society

It is commonly accepted that European invasion of the Pacific disrupted life for Pacific islanders; however, internal changes in rituals, art and politics were not uncommon before contact was established. For example, the period from the mid-1800s to the 1920s is thought by the anthropologist Bruce Knauft to have been a period of intense regional social change on the south-west coast of Papua New Guinea, influenced by a marauding and aggressive group known as the Marind or Tuger from Irian Jaya. The monolithic statues of Easter Island represent a technology and tradition which had already radically changed by the time of the earliest European explorations in the 1500s. In the villages of the northern Pacific island of Yap in Micronesia, enormous wheels of stone stand as testament to a former trading practice which flourished in the early days of contact. Certainly trading was not new to islanders, who had long since established trading networks in local goods or regional specialities. For example, Torres Strait islanders acted as 'middlemen' in coastal trade between New Guinea and Australia. Many ceremonies and status-making occasions, like the trade in *kula* valuables in the Trobriand Islands, also centred on trading practices with traditional partners across island groups.

In different parts of Oceania young men and women endured strict initiation ceremonies in order to gain mental, spiritual and physical strength and wisdom. Fighting and seafaring skills and knowledge of the land were also essential. This book includes many designs taken from clubs made of hardwoods and stone and from adzes, as well as from shields used for protection (**13, 54**).

One could also protect oneself from enemies in other ways. Sorcery, on a basic level, can be defined as knowledge used to control a person's spirit or life force. This life force, it is often believed, can be manipulated after death and, to some extent, during someone's life. If a canoe sinks on a trading voyage or a garden crop fails, the loss is not simply attributed to impersonal circumstance such as storm or drought. Instead the question is: what was the agent behind the event? Who has caused this to happen? It is thought that someone skilled in the art of sorcery can achieve many things, from success in gardening to success in war and trade. Sorcery is sometimes believed to weaken the mind of one's opponent. Some artefacts included here relate to sorcery, but the object itself may mean little without the use of the words which 'activate' it. The ability to use words is in itself an art in many parts of the Pacific.

Status in a community can be achieved in a variety of ways across Oceania. In Melanesia it is common for men to compete on equal terms for status and power. Any position of power, once attained, is tenuous and can thus be contested by others using their abilities in trade, warfare or public speaking. The source of these abilities may be seen as due to prowess in sorcery and magic. Thus the magical properties of a well-executed canoe prow-board in the Trobriand Islands might so dazzle a trading partner that he could be bewitched into accepting lower prices for his goods or giving up a treasured *kula* valuable which he might otherwise have kept (**62**). Similarly, a young man of Mount Hagen in Papua New Guinea, dressed in feathers and head ornaments and with his face and body painted for a prestigious dance, may use his knowledge of potent magic to distinguish himself from his fellow dancers, who will then praise him and give him articles of value. Indigenous trade routes across both land and sea ensured that new ideas were constantly influencing existing styles and initiating innovations, for not only were objects traded but whole rituals, songs and myths, ownership of which could be as important as the possession of objects.

In general terms, Polynesian islands are characterised by a hierarchical and hereditary social structure. For example, in Tahiti chiefs (*ari'i*) and their families enjoyed privileges which were passed down to successive generations through the male line. While their power could increase through their own achievements, extravagant autocracy was held in check by other *ari'i*, who might seek a way of limiting this power if only to protect their own. Two concepts, *mana* and *taboo*, were prevalent in structures of authority in Polynesia. *Mana* can be described as a power inherent in a person or thing: the possession of ritual strength and spiritual energy; *taboo* (or *tapu*) can be defined as a set of strict regulations designed to safeguard *mana* from pollution. It was therefore necessary to protect from contamination both people of noble rank and objects with *mana* (**2**).

Artists and audiences

The inherent power of certain objects meant that access to them was restricted. In Melanesia bull-roarers were (and are) both sacred and secret things, often kept hidden (**68**). Possessions of the nobility in New Zealand were kept out of sight and above the contaminating substance of the ground. To ensure restricted access special areas, often places with mythical importance, were demarcated – men's houses, chief's places, geographical formations and forest areas were outlined with carved or painted poles. Uluru (Ayers Rock) in central Australia is one example. The form and architecture of these places, such as the Polynesian *marae*, were often spectacular, and buildings were dramatically painted or carved. The interior might be reserved for display of more sacred knowledge. In the Micronesian island of Belau, for example, the interior gables of the impressive men's houses were painted to illustrate the stories and history of the village. In western Polynesia these structures were frequently carved in hardwoods, with unpainted exteriors. Maori meeting houses had dramatically carved exteriors and interiors (**3**); men's houses in Melanesia, particularly in the Sepik area of Papua New Guinea, are sometimes spectacularly colourful in their decoration. On Papua New Guinea's south-west coast men's houses, left unadorned, were immensely long, cone-shaped structures, sometimes measuring 20 m high at their entrance and tapering to a height of just 3 m. Inside were hung the men's ancestor boards and other sacred and ceremonial objects (**69**). Such buildings were the work of many people, overseen by specialists or elders versed in the ritual order of construction and in the ceremonies which pertained to each part of the building.

In Melanesia an artisan class was uncommon. Instead, young men and women would be required to learn a craft either as part of growing up or during initiation. In Polynesia skilled men were highly trained in the production of certain artefacts, such as implements of war (**28**). This was in keeping with the spiritual importance of such objects, since the object itself was often both a source of *mana* and a reflection of the *mana* of its owner. For example, *mana* could be expressed through the successful use of a weapon in battle. With each successful performance the object reflected both its own innate *mana* and that of its owner (**8**). On some Maori ceremonial adzes the edges of the blade are notched, as a memory aid for a chief in reciting his genealogy. The detailed history of such an adze would also be known by the chief's people.

Crafts such as weaving on looms and plaiting with leaf and wood fibre were traditionally the domain of women in the Pacific, and these arts were much less subject to ritual constraints than were those of men. The patterns within the weaves and plaits show the inventiveness and skill of the makers of mats, skirts, fans and baskets (**35, 94, 95**). While the overall design of the weaves and plaits is often related to a particular region or village, there is also individuality within each style. In Polynesia, women's work included the manufacture of barkcloth or *tapa*, made by beating bark fibres together. Again, the styles can be linked to particular islands, but with a certain amount of variety evident in the design and working of the motifs within the pattern. Hawaiian barkcloth differs from that of neighbouring islands in the use of bamboo stamps to achieve a pattern (**31**).

In Micronesia, weaving was more popular. Intricate multicoloured patterns were made from threads of banana fibre, with designs passed down over generations (**38**). Plaiting is more common in Melanesia where pandanas leaves, coconut or bark fibres are selected, trimmed, dried and sometimes dyed before the complicated process of plaiting. The patterns on mats and baskets are achieved both through the particular plaits chosen and through the use of dyes. Today synthetic fibres are often incorporated or used in place of local materials to create vibrant and striking decorations (**52, 53**). In Micronesia, Melanesia and Polynesia these designs travelled through trade both before and after contact with Europeans.

Unlike the names of the collectors of Oceanic art in Western museums, the names of the artists were not generally known until more recent times, when students of these cultures became concerned with the processes of manufacture as well as the products. However, the manufacture of an item can be seen to have more than one author: often inspiration for and creation of an object is seen to come directly from a mythical source. Some objects are regarded simply as too powerful to have been created by human beings.

Art

The phrases 'Stone Age culture' and 'primitive art' have often been used in relation to Oceania. This does not mean that the peoples of the Pacific are somehow at the base of the evolutionary scale, as was commonly thought in the nineteenth century. Rather, the term Stone Age refers to a sophisticated use of tools made of stone, shell, bone and wood. The complexity of many of the designs illustrated here and the smooth surfaces achieved on hard stone are a testament to the skill, dexterity and technical abilities of the Pacific peoples. The *kapkap* is an ornately carved breast or head ornament. The back of the *kapkap* is of polished white shell, with an intricately carved piece of turtle-shell overlay. To work the fragile and sometimes brittle material of turtle shell takes great skill (**79, 90**).

The term 'decorative art' is also used in reference to Oceanic material culture, largely because so many intricate designs are worked on utilitarian objects. However, we must be careful to avoid underestimating the importance of apparently mundane articles such as bowls, on which the design often signals that an individual piece was intended for ritual use (**59**). Some objects achieve their effect through seeming irregularity in design. Others, like New Ireland Province masks incorporating the mythic spectrum from human to animal and spiritual creatures, seem designed deliberately to confuse the eye, as open fretwork and multiple colouring combine to lead the eye from fret to fret (**74**). Solomon Islands war canoes are so intricately carved and ornamented with shell inlay that they seem almost too decorative for use, yet each element has its symbolic purpose (**83**). We should, however, be cautious in trying to assign meaning to elements of art, for 'meaning' can be quite transitory. The extent to which this is true differs from island to island, with objects being inherited, traded, discarded or destroyed. For example, some symbols and images used by Aboriginal Australian artists may be interpretable by all local Aboriginal people, others may be understood only by the relevant kinship group, and yet others may be meaningful only to the artist (**43**).

It would be easy to assume that Oceanic peoples were obsessed with decorating the surfaces of their objects, even their own bodies on occasion: tattooing – intricate, personal, sometimes spiritually powerful and inevitably transitory – is one art that can cover the entire body. However, form is also an important component of Oceanic aesthetics. Form, gloss and patina of the surface are all important components of an object's beauty. This is particularly important with the human form, where tattooing, paint and oils may achieve the desired effect. Many objects of stone and wood also have a highly polished surface, colour or gloss (**32**).

The shapes of objects vary – triangular adze heads, rectangular stools and headrests, rounded bowls raised on as many as ten legs – and may relate to power. In the Highlands of Papua New Guinea, for example, pearl-shell crescents can be important indicators of a man's skill and abilities in the competitive giving of gifts; prized shell pieces will sometimes have a red patina on their surface. In Polynesia, ownership of the finely polished teeth of pigs or whales, strung together, was once restricted to those of chiefly or royal descent (**13**). The elegant curves of Polynesian headrests were also reserved for the heads of noblemen or kings. Although it was once thought that this was to protect their elaborate hairstyles during sleep, it is perhaps more likely that it was so as not to tarnish their extensive *mana* by contact with the ground.

The principal colours used to decorate wooden artefacts are red, yellow, black and white. Black and white are both vital shades in Melanesian colour systems. Black is often used to denote anger, danger and strength, while white may symbolise death or brightness; in Polynesia, red is a colour related to the deities. The rich red of the Hawaiian feathered cloaks, for example, reflects their importance (**30**).

Many objects illustrated in this book relate to dancing. At large feasts or private events this usually involves the dancers being dressed in particular ornaments, head-dresses and with their torsos painted or oiled. Half-celebratory, some dances were also extravagant displays of the wealth and strength of the host group. Today many Pacific peoples participate in the four-yearly Pacific Arts Festival as well as more localised inter-island competitive dancing. Dancing is not always a celebration or a demonstration of unity; it can be intrinsic to serious and harsh initiation periods, or may be enacted not for a worldly audience but in a ritual context, such as for a death. Often this requires the use of masks, as in New Britain, where masks made of barkcloth were associated with the well-being of children. Masks were not used in isolation: they were often part of a dance costume which might also include colourful glossy leaves and flowers, armbands, legbands, shell and beaded necklaces, woven bags and cloth, barkcloth, feathers, hair styles, tattoos, body paints and oils, skirts of grass, bark or leaf, animal fur, head-dresses and ear and nose ornaments. Not all dances use masks, as these may be thought to transform the wearer into another state; such a transformation would be highly inappropriate for an occasion at which uninitiated people might be present.

Conclusion

For those who wish to draw their own inspiration from the pieces depicted in this book, it could be useful to try to copy the designs as a way to retrain one's eye in looking at detail. Turning to an Austral Islands paddle, for example, one can see the simplification of human forms – arms and legs akimbo, hands joined – within the geometric patterns (**25**). Some seemingly repetitive forms actually contain multiple irregularities. It is worth remembering that these works represent a moment in history. We know very little about the work created a hundred years before the first European ships sailed into the region – but there are many changes to be seen from the hundred years since. For example, Cook Islands adzes (**23**) are thought to have been produced in greater numbers in order to take advantage of the new trading opportunities.

The Pacific is made up of various cultural groups, and diversity – in design, style, materials and techniques – is found not just from one end to the other of this vast ocean, but from village to village. I have tried to draw attention to some of the general features of Pacific society and art in this brief introduction, but it is well to keep in mind that although the designs in this book illustrate the arts of the Pacific, there are at least as many ways of seeing or understanding aesthetic principles as there are objects included here. Some, such as carved wooden bowls, follow a strict form, and it is the overall shape which captures the eye. Others may seem more fanciful or free-flowing in their design, but here too a definite, if different, symmetry can be seen. Yet others are so filled with regular and geometric detail that they seem useless as practical objects. Some weapons, for example, may look lethal but are so heavy that they would be impossible to use in war. They are valuable items, prized for their aesthetic essence and their innate power, which may be genealogical, so that each owner is 'blessed' by its presence. The people who made these objects created such works both within their own traditions and for trading outside, following past principles and traditions in design and aesthetics but at the same time encompassing innovations and individual styles.

JUDE LLOYD

Notes on the Designs

All drawings are of objects, artefacts and textiles from the collections of the Ethnographic Department of the British Museum. The registration number of each object is given after its description and size.

Polynesia – New Zealand – Aotearoa

The Maori people live on the islands of New Zealand. As a result of the close relationship between Britain and New Zealand throughout the colonial period Maori artefacts are well represented in British collections, including the ethnographic collections of the British Museum. The Maori excelled in carving and shaping objects from wood, bone and nephrite, a highly valued green coloured stone also called jade. The stylised human form – with the mouth open and tongue projecting in an attitude of defiance, three- or four-fingered hands, extensive tattoo-like markings and depiction of the sexual organs – is characteristic of many designs.

1 Paddles (*hoe*) are carved from one piece of wood and have a long handle opening out into a leaf-shaped blade. The utilitarian paddles are usually plain with a small decorative area carved into the handle butt and shoulder. TOP RIGHT is the *manaia* (profile) of the TOP LEFT figure. Length of paddle TOP LEFT and RIGHT 225 cm; 5372. BOTTOM 170 cm; 1944.Oc.2.798.

2 TOP LEFT *Hei tiki* of bone with inlaid pearl-shell eyes. The *hei tiki* are highly valued heirlooms; some have their own names, personal stories and *mana* (spiritual energy). Height 9.8 cm; 1922.6-7.1. TOP RIGHT *Hei tiki* representing a female, said to be worn to promote fertility and easy childbirth. Carved in nephrite. Height 13.8 cm; S.825. BOTTOM LEFT *Hei matau*, a fish-hook shaped nephrite pendant said to be a symbol of special knowledge. Width 8.2 cm; 1944.Oc.2.829. BOTTOM CENTRE Nephrite pendant with a flax cord and bone toggle (not illustrated). This unique *hei tiki* was given in the 1830s to a Captain Sadler by the Ngapuhi chief Titore. Length 8.5 cm; 96-925. BOTTOM RIGHT *Koropepe* (coiled eel-like animal) nephrite pendant. Length 5.5 cm; 1934.12-5.29.

3 TOP LEFT Carving in wood with reddish dye from a Maori store house. Store houses were built to protect food stores from rats or to protect heirlooms. Elaborately carved store houses and meeting houses became a feature of post-colonial Maori life (Phelps 1975: 25). Height 56 cm; Q81.Oc.1440. TOP CENTRE One of two wood figures carved back-to-back, representing the partnership of the Treaty of Waitangi which established British colonial sovereignty over New Zealand in 1840. This figure, holding a quill, represents the *pakeha* (Europeans); another on the reverse side (not illustrated) represents the Maori people. Height 93 cm; Oc.1990.L.1.1. TOP RIGHT Carved detail from a Maori meeting house. Figures such as this represent individual ancestors, recognisable by their distinctive tattoos or features. The small figure between the legs represents succeeding generations. The meeting house is a focus of Maori identity and prestige and the carvings show the ancestors as present and vigilant; such figures are usually portrayed as strong and powerful, like this male warrior holding his *wahaika* (club). Height 142.5 cm; 94.7-16.2. BOTTOM Section of a carved wooden canoe prow showing openwork spirals. Length 172.5 cm; 1927.11-12.1.

4 The canoe bailer is of uniform shape across the Pacific. Maori bailers (*tata*) are recognisable by their elegant form and their carving, which is restricted to the handle and edge. TOP LEFT Canoe bailer, showing upwardly curved handle and carved decoration. Length of bailer 40 cm; 1944.Oc.2.802. TOP RIGHT Carved decoration from wooden bailer. Length of bailer 42 cm; 55.12-20.70. BOTTOM Detail of carved decoration from wooden bailer. Length of bailer 42 cm; 55.12-20.70.

5 In older utilitarian *hoe*, carved detail was restricted to the butt and shoulder of the paddle. Some *hoe* were elaborately decorated and used by the coxswain as devices to mark time to canoe chants (Phelps 1975: 27). TOP LEFT Detail of carved decoration on a model paddle. Length 84 cm; 48.3-13.2. CENTRE Carved wooden paddle. Length 194 cm; NZ149. BOTTOM Face carved on a wooden flute. Length of flute 53 cm; Q81.Oc.1.629.

6 As *wakahuia* (treasure boxes) were used to contain personal valuables worn on the body and imbued with the *tapu* of the wearer, it was important to hang the treasure box away from possible polluting elements. For this reason it was often the underside of the *wakahuia* that was most ornately carved. With increasing European trade the lids of 'tourist' *wakahuia* became more ornate to suit their new uses. TOP and CENTRE Carving on lid and side of treasure box. Length 45 cm; 1926.3-13.30. BOTTOM Carving on lid of treasure box. Length 46.5 cm; 2715.

7 TOP Lid of carved wooden *wakahuia* (treasure box). Length 37 cm; 94.272. BOTTOM *Wakahuia* (treasure box) lid. Length 52 cm; 96.11-19.3.

8 Maori weapons reflect the pre-colonial practice of hand-to-hand combat in warfare. Hand-held clubs were well suited to small-scale fighting. The small hole drilled into the base of the handle of many of these clubs would have held a wrist cord so that the weapon was not lost during combat. Weapons carried *mana* and so care was taken to hang them in safety from the rafters and walls of the house. The clubs of successful warriors were highly valued heirlooms and, like many Maori objects, the club itself may have received a name and a history through successive generations (Phelps 1975: 31; D'Alleva 1990: 34). TOP LEFT *Kotiate*, a type of hand club, carved in wood. Length 39 cm; Q87.Oc.35. TOP CENTRE *Wahaika* (bone hand club). The name means 'fish mouth'. Length 35.8 cm; 1934.2.12.1. TOP RIGHT *Maripi* (wooden knife) edged with sharks' teeth, used for cutting meat. The design shows a *manaia* (figure in profile) biting into and grasping the cutting edge. Length 24 cm; 54.12-29.9. BOTTOM Whale-bone *heru* or combs. LEFT Length 33 cm; NZ163. RIGHT Length 22.6 cm; +6159.

9 *Wahaika* and *mere* (ovoid hand club). Hand clubs were another type of object which appealed to European buyers, and some more ornate weapons may have been made for this trade. TOP LEFT Bone *wahaika*. Length 40 cm; NZ88. TOP CENTRE *Wahaika* of wood, purchased in 1868. Length 32 cm; 9331. TOP RIGHT Bone *mere* collected in 1900. Length 41 cm; TRH11. BOTTOM LEFT Wood *wahaika*. Length 36.8 cm; 1696. BOTTOM RIGHT Wood *wahaika*. Length 39.5 cm; 54.12-29.55.

10 *Mere, patu* and *kotiate* hand clubs. TOP LEFT Wooden hand club. Length 41 cm; 95-362. CENTRE Detail from a hand club. Length 27 cm; 6726. RIGHT Wooden hand club. Length 30 cm; 1925.5-9.1. BOTTOM LEFT Bone hand club. Length 39 cm; 95-363. RIGHT *Kotiate*. Length 32 cm; 1934.12-1.27.

11 *Taiaha* (staff). When ornamented with flax and feathers, *taiaha* were also used by men of rank as oratory staffs (Phelps 1975: 31). TOP LEFT Detail of *taiaha* handle. Length 179 cm; 931. LEFT CENTRE Detail showing side of *taiaha* handle. Length 168 cm; 54.12-29.76. RIGHT CENTRE Detail of *taiaha* handle. Length 167 cm; 1908.5-13.4. RIGHT Detail of back of *taiaha* handle. Length 141 cm; +3561.

12 Maori artists and craftspeople continue to make pieces in the Maori style, often in new materials such as pottery along with traditional materials like nephrite. Maori women sometimes wear belts and headbands woven from natural or synthetic materials for dances and formal occasions. TOP A black and yellow woven belt from Ruatoria, East Cape, New Zealand. Length 96.5 cm; 1994.Oc.4.79. TOP LEFT, TOP RIGHT and CENTRE Designs from a pottery ball. Height 7 cm; 1994.Oc.4.86. BOTTOM LEFT *Pekapeka*, nephrite pendant in the form of a flying bat. Carved for the British Museum by Clem Mellish of Havelock, Marlborough, New Zealand. Width 10.2 cm; 1994.Oc.4.102A. BOTTOM RIGHT Whalebone pendant carved by Jonathan Mohi Moke from Ruatoria, East Cape, New Zealand. Length

11.5 cm; 1994.Oc.4.82. BOTTOM Woven headband from Ruatoria, East Cape. Length 26 cm; 1994.Oc.4.78.

Melanesia – Fiji

The Fijian Islands of Melanesia lie on the boundary of Polynesia. Fijian artefacts are often included in Polynesian collections because of the many similarities between the material culture and societies of the two regions. The fine quality of Fijian work in wood, bone and barkcloth was recognised many centuries ago by the neighbouring Tongan Islanders, who travelled to Fiji's western islands to purchase goods. From 1879 there has been a growing Indian population, originally brought over as indentured labour, and today roughly half the population of the islands is of Indian descent.

13 TOP LEFT *Ula*, a Fijian throwing club called *Iula tavatava*, meaning 'fluted head'. This type of club could be used in warfare or hunting; the patterned area at the base of the club was aimed to hit the prey, the bulbous end lending weight to the throw. Length 44 cm; 975. CENTRE *Civa* (whalebone breast ornaments) were once restricted to men of great rank. Their rarity and value was quickly understood by Europeans, who imported large quantities of bone for trade and barter. This *civa* may date from the internal political fighting of the mid 1800s (it was obtained during the 'little war' in Fiji from a Rewa warrior, who took it at the sacking of Mala navali). Width 19 cm; 1931.7-14.33. TOP RIGHT Carved decoration on the centre of a wooden club. Length of club 99 cm; 1944.Oc.2.1018. BOTTOM LEFT *Civa* with shell inlay. The colour of the whalebone is a rich egg yellow, inset with greyish polished shell. The fine fit between the two is a testament to the skill of the craftsman. Diameter 20.5 cm; 1931.7-14.32. BOTTOM RIGHT *Civa* made from whalebone pieces held together with fine pegs at the back. Diameter 22.5 cm; 1934.12-5.31.

14 The pattern on Fijian barkcloth or *masi* is made by using a stencil over which the dye is rubbed, creating the strong central motifs. Additional border patterning is created by rubbing over smaller stencils. In the interior of Viti Levu stencils were made from bamboo cylinders which were engraved and rolled over the beaten white cloth. The predominant colouring is white, brown/red and brown/black. Fiji is one of the few Pacific nations to have maintained its tradition of barkcloth production. TOP Black, brown and white *masi*. Length of piece 96 cm; 89.3-2.4. BOTTOM Black, brown/red and white *masi*, presented to the British Museum in 1895. Length of piece 47 cm; 95-147.

15 Stencils or printing blocks (*kupeti*) for barkcloth designs. The stencil would be placed on a board before rubbing dye into the barkcloth. TOP LEFT Length 44 cm; 1920.3-22.25. TOP RIGHT Length 40.5 cm; 1920.3-22.31. TOP CENTRE Length 49 cm; 1920.3-22.26.

CENTRE Length 40.5 cm; 1920.3-22.27. BOTTOM Length 47 cm; 1928-69.

Polynesia – Wallis and Futuna

The islands of Wallis, Futuna and Alofi are an overseas territory of France, although prior to colonisation they were not a single political unit. Many of the barkcloth designs from the territory are significantly similar to designs on woven rush mats from the Marshall Islands, some 3000 km away. Before Europeans came the islanders, like many other Pacific peoples, were already in contact with each other, travelling great distances in canoes and trading and influencing each other in their materials and designs (Thomas 1995: 144).

16 TOP Barkcloth detail. Width of whole cloth 190 cm; 56.7-9.14. BOTTOM Detail from barkcloth. Width of sample 34 cm; +6897.

17 TOP Barkcloth. Length of whole cloth 164 cm; 1954.Oc.6.312. BOTTOM Barkcloth. Width of whole cloth 132 cm; 1954.Oc.6.311.

Polynesia – Samoa

18 LEFT Wooden club with carved decoration infilled with lime. Length 56 cm; 94-433. CENTRE Wooden club with carved decoration. Length 68.5 cm; 1954.Oc.6.337. RIGHT Wooden club with carved decoration. Length 95 cm; LMS177.

19 Samoan barkcloth is decorated by placing a design tablet under a length of bleached cloth which is then rubbed with dye to bring out the design. Patterns may also be painted freehand on to the cloth. TOP Decorated barkcloth stamped with black, dark brown and beige designs. Length of sample 110 cm; CC5873. BOTTOM LEFT Decorated barkcloth in black, brown and white, dating from 1880. Length of sample 72 cm; 178. BOTTOM RIGHT Barkcloth with black, white and brown decoration, said to have been given to the donor by King Malietoa. Length of sample 74 cm; 87.12-17.12.

Polynesia – Niue

20 Painted barkcloth, black on beige. The floral and vine motifs accompanied by geometric patterning are typical. Width 57 cm; 1953.Oc.T.3.

21 TOP Painted barkcloth, black on beige (see **20**). Width 57 cm; 1953.Oc.T.3. BOTTOM Section of decoration on barkcloth dress, dark brown and black on beige. Samoan barkcloth techniques became popular in Niue after the London Missionary Society established a mission there. The Samoan lay preachers also introduced new ways of wearing barkcloth in dresses and ponchos (Simmons 1979: 77). This dress was purchased from the Revd J. Powell in 1866. Length of whole cloth 240 cm; 4253.

Polynesia – Cook Islands

The Cook Islands were administered by the London Missionary Society from the 1820s until 1888. This greatly affected the production of material culture – 'idolatrous' objects were destroyed or removed, although some artefacts continued to be produced for trade.

22 TOP LEFT and TOP RIGHT Two views of a 'fisherman's god' from Rarotonga. Only seven of these fishermen's gods are thought to have survived from the early nineteenth century. The figures were probably attached to canoes as a place for the god to manifest itself and aid the fisherman. The decoration may relate to tattoo patterning (Hooper 1990). Height 32 cm; 9866. CENTRE Detail of a carved wooden 'godstick' (*taaroa* or *tangaroa*). These symbols of gods were kept in houses within the restricted area of the *marae* (an open court). Length 80 cm; LMS168.

23 Details from the handles of carved wooden ceremonial adzes. This type of adze (*toki*) from Mangaia Island is ceremonial and may have been used to invoke Tane Mata Ariki, the god of carpenters, or it could have been the property of a chief. Some adzes were also produced as curios (Simmons 1979: 81). TOP Length of adze 93 cm; EP57. CENTRE Length 106 cm; 8013. BOTTOM Length 123 cm; 82.

24 TOP LEFT and TOP RIGHT A wood and stone ceremonial adze from the Cook Islands and a detail of it. The lashing on this adze is typically fine and ornate. It may be that this adze comes from Mangaia (see **23**). Length 69 cm; +8488.

French Polynesia – Austral Islands

24 BOTTOM LEFT Detail of engraved decoration on a wooden ceremonial paddle. These paddles, shaped like long-handled spoons, are usually completely covered in intricate high relief carving. Length 193 cm; LMS26. BOTTOM RIGHT Detail of engraved decoration on a wooden ceremonial paddle. Length 106.5 cm; LMS23.

25 Details from ceremonial paddles. TOP LEFT Length 126 cm; Q81.Oc.1635. TOP RIGHT Length 134 cm; Q81.Oc.162.7. CENTRE Length 117 cm; 1944.Oc.2.722. BOTTOM Detail of carved design on a wooden ceremonial adze. Length 87 cm; 7256.

French Polynesia – Society Islands – Tahiti

Of the many islands in the Leeward and Windward groups of the Society Islands, Tahiti is probably the best known; it was the site of the notorious mutiny against Captain Bligh of HMS *Bounty*. It is also the administrative capital of the group and of French Polynesia. The islands became known to Europe through the voyages of exploration in the late eighteenth century. Tahitians of high rank travelled to

Europe in the nineteenth century, where they enjoyed royal patronage and great popularity on their journeys. The striking artefacts of the Tahitians were part of the earliest displays from the Pacific to be shown in the British Museum.

26 Stone pounder. Basalt pounders were used to mash breadfruit in preparation for storing. It is possible that this pounder dates from Captain Cook's voyages (Kaeppler 1978: 149). Height 18.5 cm; TAH15. CENTRE Carved wooden canoe ornament. This interesting piece is a fine example of what could be called the 'Polynesian style': the large head and abdomen, with hands clasped over it, and the squatting position of the figures can be seen in other Polynesian works (see **22**). Length 57.5 cm; 1939.Oc.11.1. RIGHT Wooden handle of a fly whisk. Fly whisks were symbols of rank and prestige in eastern Polynesia. Length 69 cm; TAH137.

27 Barkcloth (*tapa*) was made by women in Tahiti and used as a prestige object, for clothing and for bedding. The leaf-print designs are made by applying a dye-soaked fern leaf or petal to the sun-bleached barkcloth. TOP Decorated barkcloth garment with leaf-print design. Length 253 cm; TAH102. BOTTOM LEFT Detail of leaf-print design on a barkcloth robe. Length of robe 137 cm; 1983. BOTTOM RIGHT Detail of leaf-print design on barkcloth. Length of cloth 234 cm; 1922.11-11.2.

French Polynesia – Marquesas Islands

The Marquesas Islands may well have been the cradle and centre of eastern Polynesian culture (Phelps 1975: 92; Ivory in Dark 1993: 72). It is thought that the islands were settled c. 300-200 BC. The people of the ten habitable islands of the Marquesas have produced some of the most striking artefacts of the region. The motif of the face with rounded eyes and open oval mouth appears on clubs, bowls and also on the body, which in former times was extensively tattooed.

28 TOP *Uhikana*, a headband of mother of pearl shell with turtle overlay. Width 43 cm; 1903-19. BOTTOM LEFT The *'u'u* or carved wooden club is the most collected object from the Marquesas Islands (Ivory in Dark 1993). Specialist artisans called *tuhuna* carved in wood and these clubs are an excellent example of their skill. Length 138.5 cm; 1920.3-17.1. BOTTOM RIGHT Carved wooden club. Length 142 cm; 1913.237.

29 Bowls were used as food containers but also, with lids, to store valuables. Wooden lids were also carved to fit gourds. TOP *Kumate* (wooden bowl) carved with a pattern representing human faces. Diameter 28.9 cm; Q80.Oc.1066. CENTRE Carved wooden bowl or lid from Fatu Hiva Island. Length 35 cm; 99-157. BOTTOM Wooden lid of box. Length 38 cm; 1954.Oc.6.362.

Polynesia – Hawaii

Feathered cloaks and capes were made only in Hawaii and New Zealand. In Hawaii they were constructed of small bunches of feathers attached to a fisherman's knot netting (*olona*). They were largely restricted to higher chiefs as a mark of social distinction and rank. In Polynesia red was the symbolic colour of high chiefs and associated with the gods. Although the name *'ahu'ula* means 'red garment', they were also made of rare yellow *'o'o* and *mamo* feathers as well as the red feathers of the *i'iwi* and *'apapane* birds.

30 TOP LEFT *'Ahu'ula* (feather cape) of yellow *'o'o* and black and red *i'iwi* feathers on a fibre net (*olona*). Width 73 cm; HAW135. TOP RIGHT *'Ahu'ula* of yellow, black and red feathers. Width 129 cm; 1903.L.1.4. CENTRE LEFT *'Ahu'ula* of yellow and red feathers. Width 201 cm; 1903.L.1.2. CENTRE RIGHT *'Ahu'ula* of yellow *'o'o* and red *i'iwi* feathers with black. Width 87 cm; 1903.L.1.5. BOTTOM LEFT *'Ahu'ula* with red *i'iwi* feathers forming the groundwork and yellow *'o'o* and *mamo* feathers making the pattern. Width 225 cm; HAW133. BOTTOM RIGHT *'Ahu'ula* of red and yellow. Width 77 cm; HAW141.

31 TOP RIGHT Barkcloth piece from the Meyrick collection with black and red patterning on white. It was not uncommon for barkcloth to be cut into samples and bound into books in European collections. These books are invaluable for those interested in the variety and complexity of Polynesian barkcloth designs. Width of piece 38.5 cm; 78.11-1.603. CENTRE LEFT Patterning from a gourd. Height of gourd 37 cm; 1548. BOTTOM Plaited leaf fan or *peahi*. This shape was made for chiefs. The handles were often embroidered with human hair and dyed fibres to create distinctive zig-zag patterns. Width 47 cm; LMS200.

Polynesia – Easter Island – Rapa Nui

32 TOP LEFT White painted stone with bird-man carved in low relief. Bird-man petroglyphs can still be seen at the important ceremonial site of Orongo on Easter Island. Width 39 cm; 1920.5-6.1. CENTRE Detail of the decoration on an ancestor figure (see **33**). The designs may relate to tribal affiliations (Simmons 1979: 92). Length 46 cm; EP20. RIGHT *Rapa* – wooden dance paddle with a human face, evoked by a low-relief carving of a line representing eyebrows and a nose. Such paddles were twirled between the fingers during dances. Length 82 cm; +2600. BOTTOM LEFT This head forms the top of a *ua* used as a staff, carried by chiefs as a symbol of authority. These long staffs are made of beautifully smooth red wood. The almond eyes, stylised ears and hair are typical of Easter Island design. Length 152 cm; 203.

33 TOP ROW Wooden carvings from Easter Island. LEFT Fish-shaped wooden carving. Length 37.5 cm; EP30. CENTRE LEFT *Moai kavakava* or male ancestor figure.

These emaciated figures, carved from wood, are a feature of Easter Island art. The head is decorated with intricate carvings (see **32**). Some figures are pierced at the back of the neck for suspension in order to be worn at feasts and ceremonial occasions. Length 43.5 cm; EP21. CENTRE RIGHT Carved wooden male ancestor figure (see **32**). Length 46 cm; EP20. RIGHT *Moai moko*, a figure of a fish-man carved in wood. These figures may have been positioned to guard house entrances or worn by dancers during festivals. Length 41.5 cm; EP29. BOTTOM *Rei miro*, a wooden breast ornament with two incised symbols. These were worn by men of rank. Width 69 cm; 6847.

Polynesia – Tonga

The kingdom of Tonga, consisting of forty-five inhabited islands, is Polynesia's oldest and last surviving kingdom.

34 TOP LEFT Incised decoration from a carved wooden club, probably Tongan. Traditionally made by special craftsmen (*tufunga*) using sharks' teeth as engraving tools, Tongan clubs are usually completely covered in zig-zag and line motifs between strong parallel lines (Phelps 1975: 163). Length 99 cm; 153. TOP RIGHT Detail of carved decoration on a wooden club. Length 115 cm; 55.12-20.77. BOTTOM LEFT Decoration on a bamboo flute, probably from Tonga. Length 58.5 cm; Q80.Oc.1114. BOTTOM CENTRE These discs or baffles have hooks attached for hanging food away from rodents. The decorations are similar to Tongan food hooks collected on Captain Cook's second voyage (1772–5) (Kaeppler: 224). Diameter 24 cm; Q80.Oc.1199. BOTTOM RIGHT Designs from the end of a basket. Height of basket 20.5 cm; Q80.Oc.1127.

Micronesia – Marshall Islands

Literally meaning 'little islands', the term Micronesia well describes this area – the size of the United States – which is dotted with over two thousand islands. The peoples of the hundred inhabited islands in the former Trust Territory of the Pacific Islands, which includes the Marshall and Caroline Islands, do not share a common linguistic or cultural heritage.

35 Woven mats. TOP to BOTTOM: Length 92 cm; 1976.Oc.9.6. Length 92 cm; 1938.10-1.62. Length 92 cm; 1976.Oc.9.6. Length 83 cm; 7267. Length 92 cm; 1938.10-1.63.

Micronesia – Belau

36 The Republic of Belau or Palau is the most eastern of the Micronesian Islands, lying 800 km east of the Philippines. TOP LEFT Lid of wooden bowl with shell inlay. Diameter 15 cm; Q87.Oc.95. TOP RIGHT Lid of wooden bowl with shell inlay. Diameter 16 cm; 75.10-2.2. BOTTOM Wooden bowl with shell inlay. Height 20 cm; 75.10-2.2.

37 TOP RIGHT Wooden bowl with shell inlay. Diameter 15 cm; Q87.Oc.95. CENTRE Wooden sword with shell inlay. Length 81 cm; 75.10-2.3. BOTTOM LEFT Container for traditional money. Wood with shell inlay. Presented by Revd W. S. Simpson in 1879. Height 10 cm; 5979.

Micronesia – Pohnpei Island

The Pohnpei Islanders are one of the few Pacific groups to practise loom weaving. Belts were made from threads of banana fibre which, once dyed, were arranged in strips and woven, with the warp threads providing the patterns. The blocks illustrated (see **38** and **39**) were carved in wood for a Mr Christian by Alek of Panatik, south-eastern Pohnpei, to show some of the decorative patterns used on the islands.

38 TOP Length 29.5 cm; 99-22. BOTTOM LEFT Length 14.2 cm; 99-30. BOTTOM RIGHT Length 24 cm; 99-26.

39 TOP Length 23 cm; 99-25. BOTTOM LEFT Length 15 cm; 99-31. BOTTOM RIGHT Length 18.5 cm; 99-29.

Micronesia – Mortlock Islands

40 Decorated wooden dance paddles. From LEFT to RIGHT : Length 98 cm; +5973. Length 118 cm; 99-43a. Length 116 cm; 99-43. Double-ended dance paddles: Length 161 cm; +5972. Length 105 cm; 99-44.

Australia – Western Australia

The culture and art of the Aboriginal people of Australia form the longest continuous tradition in the world, dating back around fifty millennia. Despite the vastness of the continent there are common elements in the diverse Aboriginal traditions, which centre on what has become known as the 'Dreaming'. The Dreaming describes the epic deeds and activities of supernatural beings and ancestors who created the known Aboriginal world and made laws governing social and religious behaviour. Art is linked to this religious domain and is a means of connecting the present with the past (Caruana 1993: 7-14).

41 Engravings from baobab nuts showing animal and human images. The nuts from the bulbous baobab tree are extremely hard, making them ideal for engraving. TOP LEFT and BOTTOM RIGHT Engraved baobab nut from the Broome area, north Western Australia, showing a small marsupial on its hind legs. Collected in 1896. Length 15 cm; 96-1048. TOP RIGHT and CENTRE LEFT Engraved bird, Western Australia. Length 21 cm; 1942.Oc.3.2. CENTRE, CENTRE RIGHT and BOTTOM LEFT Three engravings on one baobab nut, from Port Darwin, Western Australia. Length 20 cm; 1933.3-15.21. BOTTOM CENTRE Engraved lizards from Kimberley District, Western Australia. Length 19 cm; 1939.Oc.12.3.

42 Engraved pearl-shell pubic covers, or phallocrypts. The symbolic designs, including a geometric maze, are incised on the highly polished shell surface and then infilled with red ochre. The polished and sometimes engraved pearl shells were traded inland from the coast and highly valued. TOP LEFT From Cossack, Hammersley Range. Length 17.4 cm; 96-1041. TOP RIGHT From Kimberley District. Length 18.5 cm; 1954.Oc.6.376. BOTTOM Worora Tribe. Length 14 cm; 1935.4-13.3.

43 Engraved pearl-shell pubic covers (phallocrypts). TOP LEFT From Kimberley District. Length 16.8 cm; 1954.Oc.6.378. TOP From Kimberley District. Length 16.8 cm; 1954.Oc.6.377. BOTTOM LEFT From Cossack, Hammersley Range. Length 12.5 cm; 96-1042. BOTTOM RIGHT From north Western Australia. Length 11 cm; 95-68.

Australia – Queensland

The painted wooden shields from the rainforests of north-eastern Queensland are distinctive for their designs and colours. Traditionally two initiated men would paint the shield together, using broad bands and blocks of colour in red, white and yellow with black outlines defining the patterns. Although the symmetrical designs symbolise objects used in everyday life as well as plants and animals, they also relate to wider religious themes. Shields like these were traditionally used in initiation and warfare (Caruana 1993: 170).

44 LEFT Red, white and black painted wooden shield, Cairns District. Length 79 cm; 1931.11-18.33. RIGHT Red, yellow, white and black painted wooden shield, Cairns District. Length 87 cm; 1933.4-3.3.

45 Wooden shields painted with red, white, yellow and black pigment, Cairns District. LEFT Length 129 cm; +2461. CENTRE Length 100 cm; 7696. RIGHT Length 87 cm; 1933.4-3.8.

Australia – Northern Territory

With the growing international market in Aboriginal art, painters from the Northern Territory have tended to favour non-secret and new designs in their works. Traditional *tjukurrpa* (paintings) from Arnhemland refer to specific Dreamtime stories. The right to reproduce these stories is restricted by gender, descent, age, initiation and status (Megaw and Megaw in Dark 1993: 163-4). In north-eastern Arnhemland paintings can be a conceptualised map of a clan's land boundaries and also reflect their ancestors' stories (Caruana 1993: 59).

46 Detail of *mana* (ancestral shark) from a bark painting by Djutja Djutja, north-eastern Arnhemland. Length of whole painting 174 cm; 1986.Oc.7.5. BOTTOM Detail of magpie geese from a bark painting in black, white and browns, from Ramingining. Length of whole painting 236 cm; 1989.Oc.5.1.

47 TOP Bark painting showing kangaroos in black,

yellow and red, from Ramingining. Length 142 cm; 1989.Oc.5.4. CENTRE Detail of two long-necked tortoises from a black, brown and white bark painting by Dorothy Djukulul, Ramingining. Length 69 cm; 1989.Oc.5.1.1. BOTTOM Fish painted on bark in brown and white, from Arnhemland, Northern Territory. The use of cross-hatching and continuous lines, as in this depiction of a fish, expresses visual brilliance, an important religious aesthetic in some Aboriginal painting (Carauana 1993: 60). Length 22.5 cm; 1960.Oc.8.1.

Australia – Torres Strait Islands

The Torres Strait Islanders live on the islands in the strait which separates New Guinea and Australia. A seafaring people, much of their art and material culture relates to the sea. They have been particularly adept at modelling huge images from turtle-shell, as well as making smaller ornaments with incised decoration.

48 TOP LEFT *Sabagorar*, double fish-hook bridal ornament collected by A. C. Haddon in 1889 from Mer Island. Length 16 cm; 89+38. TOP CENTRE Fish pendant from Mer Island, collected by A. C. Haddon in 1889. Length 7 cm; 89+110. TOP RIGHT Fish-hook pendant, 1870. Length 15 cm; 6938. BOTTOM *Sabagorar*, double fish-hook bridal ornament, collected by A. C. Haddon in 1889. Width 18.5 cm; 89+253.

Indonesia – Irian Jaya – North Coast

The coastal people of Irian Jaya have been expert traders for many centuries. Traders from other Indonesian islands and Malaysia came to the Irian Jayan coast for local products such as feathers, dried fish and woods, which were exchanged for glass beads, textiles and metals. In turn the coastal people could use these imported trade items to obtain products from the interior and to forge lasting trade relationships between villages. It is perhaps these long-established trade networks which have led to the unique style of the north coast (Rice 1991: 276).

49 Headrests were used in the men's houses in the Geelvink (Cenderawasih) Bay area, and among the Waropen people in marriage exchange. TOP LEFT Carved wooden headrest from Geelvink Bay. Width 22 cm; +3833. TOP RIGHT Carved wooden headrest. Width 33 cm; 65.5-3.2. CENTRE Carved wooden canoe prow ornament. The Humboldt Bay area, where this ornament comes from, is close to the border of Papua New Guinea, but its art reflects the long-standing contact with Indonesians from the Moluccas Islands. Canoes were important and prow ornaments often incorporated images such as this bird-man for guidance and protection (Rice 1991: 268). Length 38 cm; 1954.Oc.6.12. BOTTOM Carved wooden headrest from Doreh, Geelvink Bay. Length 62 cm; 65.5-3.1.

50 TOP LEFT Carved wooden canoe prow ornament

from Humboldt Bay. Width 38.8 cm; 1944.Oc.2.2039. TOP RIGHT *Korwar* (ancestor figures) were usually carved by the deceased relatives' kin as a mark of respect and for use as a kind of oracle (Rice 1991: 269). Trade goods such as cloth and glass beads were often incorporated into the *korwar*. From Geelvink Bay. Height 40 cm; 1961.Oc.4.1. BOTTOM LEFT Carved 'shield' from a *korwar* (ancestor figure) collected in 1859 from Doreh, Geelvink Bay. Length 23.3 cm; 1935.10-14.6. BOTTOM RIGHT *Korwar* (ancestor figure) with typical scroll-like carving on the 'shield'. From Doreh, Geelvink Bay. Length 28 cm; 65.5-3.3.

Melanesia – Papua New Guinea

More than seven hundred languages are spoken in Papua New Guinea, a linguistic variety which hints at the cultural and artistic diversity of this large island. For ease of description objects have been divided into regional and island groups.

51 Engraved coconut containers. TOP LEFT From eastern Madang. Height 12 cm; 1929-25. TOP RIGHT and BOTTOM Two views of a coconut container from East Tami. Height 10.5 cm; +5885.

Melanesia – Papua New Guinea – Western Highlands Province

Not until the 1930s did the first European explorers reach the highland regions of Papua New Guinea. Today the area of Mount Hagen and the surrounding hills and valleys are easily accessible by air and the highland people have made use of new materials in their material culture, as these net-bags demonstrate. Inter-clan fighting has also changed with the introduction of firearms; for instance shields, once made of wood for protection against spears, are now often made of metal.

52 *Bilum* (net-bags) are used throughout much of New Guinea, and not just as containers: suspended from the forehead and worn hanging down the back, they also form part of a woman's attire. New materials and designs are continually incorporated into the fabric of what are highly expandable bags. These net-bags come from the Wahgi Valley and were collected in 1990. TOP LEFT Width 50 cm; 1990.Oc.9.91. TOP RIGHT Width 32 cm; 1990.Oc.9.93. BOTTOM LEFT Width 40 cm; 1990.Oc.9.92. BOTTOM RIGHT Width 57 cm; 1990.Oc.9.85.

53 *Bilum* from the Wahgi Valley, Western Highlands Province. TOP Width 61 cm; 1990.Oc.9.98. BOTTOM LEFT Width 44 cm; 1990.Oc.9.94. BOTTOM RIGHT Purchased in Port Moresby, and said by the seller to be an angel design. Width 41 cm; 1995.Oc.4.5.

54 LEFT The pattern on the edge of this Wahgi Valley shield is taken from the packaging of San Miguel beer. The Cambridge Cup is a rugby league competition, but here refers to inter-clan warfare. Height 163 cm;

1990.Oc.9.2. CENTRE 'Six to Six' generally denotes an all-night party; here the term is an assertion of the warriors' capacity to fight all day long. Height 165 cm; 1990.Oc.9.16. RIGHT *Nau wantok kaikai wantok* roughly translates as 'Now buddy slays buddy'. Height 159 cm; 1990.Oc.9.20.

Melanesia – Papua New Guinea – East and West Sepik

55 LEFT Painted shield from the Telefomin District, West Sepik Province, decorated in red, black and white. Height 195cm; 1988.Oc.6.6. RIGHT low relief carved shield, painted red, white and black, from Upamin, Telefomin District. Height 150 cm; 1964.Oc.3.71.

56 LEFT Carved wooden food hook painted orange, black and white, from Tambanum village, East Sepik Province. Length 73.5 cm; 1979.Oc.7.71. RIGHT Pottery bowl with engraved decoration. Diameter 34.7 cm; 1979.Oc.7.27.

57 TOP LEFT Pottery vessel painted red, black and white. Diameter 23 cm; 1980.Oc.11.273. TOP RIGHT Detail from a carved wooden headrest. Length 58 cm; 1919.7-18.28. BOTTOM LEFT Pottery vessel with red, white, black and yellow decoration. Diameter 32 cm; 1980.Oc.11.266. BOTTOM RIGHT Wooden carving painted red, yellow, black and white, from the Maprik District. Length 68 cm; 1980.Oc.11.215.

Melanesia – Papua New Guinea – Morobe District – Huon Gulf

58 Carved and painted motifs on Tami Island wooden bowls and sticks. The bowls are made from hard wood, blackened and polished on the surface, with incised patterns filled with lime and smeared with red or white. The designs, owned and controlled by the makers, were passed from one generation to the next. TOP LEFT Detail of motif on a wooden bowl. Length of bowl 50 cm; +5884. TOP and BOTTOM RIGHT Detail of face and bird from the ends of a carved wooden staff, from Tami Island. Length 48 cm; 1954.Oc.6.60. TOP CENTRE Detail of motif on a Tami Island wooden dish. Length of dish 63 cm; 1919.7-18.60. BOTTOM LEFT Carved wooden female figure collected in 1886 from Tami Island. Length 41 cm; 1954.Oc.6.62. BOTTOM CENTRE Carved motif on a wooden dish from Tami Island. Length of dish 63 cm; 1919.7-18.60.

59 Tami Island bowls were highly sought after as exchange items in New Britain in the nineteenth and twentieth centuries. TOP LEFT Decoration from a Tami Island bowl. Length 65 cm; Q78.Oc.9.6. TOP RIGHT Decoration from a Tami Island bowl. Length 50 cm; +5884. CENTRE and BOTTOM LEFT and RIGHT Three motifs from carved decoration on a bowl. Length of bowl 50 cm; +5884.

60 Carved and painted wooden headrests from Tami Island. TOP LEFT Height 17 cm; 1954.Oc.1.1. TOP RIGHT Height 16 cm; +5878. BOTTOM Height 18 cm; 1954.Oc.6.64.

61 Carved and painted wooden headrests from Tami Island. TOP LEFT Height 15 cm; 1950.Oc.4.1. TOP RIGHT Acquired in 1886. Height 14 cm; 86.10-15.27. BOTTOM Height 15 cm; 1951.Oc.13.6.

Melanesia – Papua New Guinea – Milne Bay District and the Trobriand Islands

62 TOP Carved wooden board from the Milne Bay District. Length 171 cm; 1919-438. CENTRE LEFT Canoe prow splash board from the Trobriand Islands, carved wood with white inlay. From the collection of the anthropologist Bronislaw Malinowski. Length 45 cm; 1922.M.66. CENTRE RIGHT Model canoe prow ornament from Kiriwina Island in the Trobriand group. Length 22.5 cm; 1919.149. BOTTOM Canoe prow board, probably from the Trobriand Islands. Length 58.5 cm; 1851.1-3.4.

63 Painted shields from the Trobriand Islands, made of wood with red, black and white painted surface. These shields came to the British Museum in 1893. LEFT Length 88 cm; +6315. CENTRE Length 75 cm; +6314. RIGHT Length 74 cm; +6318.

64 Betel nut, often mixed with lime and other natural flavourings and taken as a mild stimulant, is chewed throughout most of Melanesia. The lime, taken from rock or made from burnt shells, is usually stored in containers like these, sealed with a spatula designed to extract the lime from the container (see **65**). TOP LEFT and BOTTOM LEFT Trobriand Islands lime gourd, purchased for the Museum in 1867. Length 26 cm; +3825. TOP RIGHT Decoration from a Trobriand Islands lime gourd. Length 21 cm; 6350. BOTTOM RIGHT Detail of the engraved decoration on a Trobriand Islands lime gourd. Height 24 cm; +6351.

65 TOP Engraved decoration from the edge of a Trobriand Islands bowl. Length 58.5 cm; 1922.M.635. CENTRE from LEFT to RIGHT Lime spatula from Milne Bay District, carved and infilled with lime. Length 28 cm; +4625. Lime spatula ornament from the Louisade Archipelago, presented to the British Museum by the explorer Captain Owen Stanley in 1851. This imitation of a spatula has a shell-disc handle (*gabaela*). Length 22.5 cm; 51.1-3.161. Comb from the Trobriand Islands, carved with details infilled with lime. Length 22 cm; 1922.M.482. Lime spatula. Length 25 cm; 1919-215. BOTTOM Decoration from around the edge of a wooden bowl. Diameter of bowl 54 cm; +6245.

66 LEFT Carved decoration with lime inlay on a wooden club from the Milne Bay District. Length of club 91 cm; +1600. TOP CENTRE Detail of the carved and lime-infilled decoration on a wooden club from the Trobriand Islands. Length of club 62 cm; +6269. BOTTOM CENTRE Detail of the carved and lime-infilled decoration on a wooden club from the Milne Bay District. Length of club 108 cm; 1957.Oc.5.3. RIGHT The end of a wooden club from the Milne Bay District, with carved detail and lime infill. Length of club 100 cm; 9158.

67 TOP ROW from LEFT to RIGHT Lime spatula, Milne Bay District. Length 45.5 cm; 1919-232. Lime spatula, Milne Bay District. Length 41 cm; 1931.7-23.18. Lime spatula from Milne Bay District. Length 31 cm; 1931.7-22.2. Betel-nut pestle from the Trobriand Islands. Length 28.5 cm; 1939.Oc.12.18. BOTTOM ROW from LEFT to RIGHT : Lime spatula from the Trobriand Islands. Length 25 cm; +6337. Betel-nut pestle with 'bracket' design, unique to the Trobriands. Length 12.5 cm; 1939.Oc.12.21. Decorated lime spatula from Milne Bay District. Length 34 cm; 1931.7-23.1.

Melanesia – Papua New Guinea – Gulf District

Many of these objects relate to a time when enormous long houses were built along the coast for use by men. Inside were hung 'ancestor' boards, drums and other religious and fighting paraphernalia.

68 LEFT Painted and engraved black and white wooden bull-roarer. Bull-roarers, which emit a curious whirring noise when swung from a cord, were once used in connection with sorcery. From Maipu, Namau. Length 68 cm; 1951.Oc.7.7. CENTRE TOP Black painted wooden board with incised pattern infilled with lime. Length 69.5 cm; 1905.6-9.34. CENTRE BOTTOM Ceremonial wooden shield carved in low relief and painted with red, black and white. Said to be hung in men's houses, they are also called 'ancestral' shields because of their associations with ancestor spirits. From the Purari River area. Length 49 cm; 1936.7-20.14. RIGHT Painted white and red bull-roarer, with engraved pattern infilled with lime. Length 75 cm; 1951.Oc.7.6.

69 From LEFT to RIGHT Black, white and red painted shield from the northern Papuan Gulf. Length 75 cm; 87.2-7.45. Black and white *kwoi* (board) from a men's house. The face motif is typical of the Papuan Gulf. Length 100 cm; 1914.4-18.36. Red, black and white *gope* board from the Kerema area. Length 96 cm; 1906.10-13.283. Red and white board from Namau. Length 88.5 cm; 1951.Oc.7.14.

70 TOP LEFT Length 14 cm; 1951.Oc.6.1. TOP CENTRE Length 13 cm; 1919-457. TOP RIGHT Length 13.5 cm; 1919-455. BOTTOM LEFT From Elema. Length 14 cm; 1919-184. BOTTOM CENTRE Length 12.5 cm; 1919-186. BOTTOM RIGHT From the Parau River area. Length 13.5 cm; 1936.7-20.16.

Melanesia – Papua New Guinea – Manus Province

71 Lime, obtained from burnt shell, stone or rock and often mixed with betel nut, is chewed as a mild stimulant across Melanesia. It was sometimes a rare commodity. These carved wooden lime spatulas are all from Hermit Island. LEFT Length 52.6 cm; 1913.5-24.19. CENTRE LEFT Spatula with double lizard/reptile motif. Length 47.4 cm; 1913.5-24.17. CENTRE RIGHT Spatula with lizard/reptile motif. Length 34 cm; 1913.5-24.16. RIGHT Length 55 cm; 1913.5-24.18.

72 *Kapkap* (breast ornaments) are made from the giant clam shell, carefully ground down to form a disc shape which forms the background for finely worked patterns of turtle-shell. Turtle-shell, although brittle when cold, becomes malleable enough to pierce without breaking when it is gently heated. These *kapkap* were designed to be worn around the neck by men and come from Manus Province. TOP LEFT Diameter 9 cm; +256. TOP RIGHT Diameter 10.2 cm; +257. CENTRE Collected on the *Challenger* Expedition of 1878. Diameter 15 cm; +716. BOTTOM LEFT Diameter 9.5 cm; +717. BOTTOM CENTRE Collected on the *Challenger* Expedition. Diameter 10.5 cm; +256. BOTTOM RIGHT Diameter 10.2 cm; 1939.Oc.1.11.

73 *Kapkap* (breast ornament). Diameter 16 cm; 1937.10-26.1.

Melanesia – Papua New Guinea – New Ireland Province

74 TOP *Malagan* sculpture, perhaps a house or dancing ornament. New Ireland Province *malagan* sculpture is characterised by its multi-focal perspectives. Here fish and hornbill are blended together in one sculpture, and painted over in red, black and white. Width 45 cm; 84.7-28.15. CENTRE RIGHT Detail of profile view of the bird from the bird-fish *malagan* sculpture (TOP). BOTTOM LEFT Carved pattern on a wooden friction gong. These ceremonial gongs are unique to New Ireland Province and when played are said to mimic the cry of a native bird. Length 47 cm; 1923.5-12.41. BOTTOM RIGHT Red, black and white painted bird ornament. Length 24 cm; 84.7-26.16.

75 *Kapkap* (breast ornaments) appear throughout the Bismarck Archipelago. They are thought to have originated in New Ireland Province and to have been distributed along local trade routes. On *kapkap* from New Ireland Province the turtle-shell overlay is often divided into four. This design may be related to the *mataling* or 'eye of fire' found on *malagan* sculpture. TOP LEFT Diameter 8.6 cm; 1920.3-22.63. TOP RIGHT Diameter 7.7 cm; 1928.11-12.25. CENTRE From the Beasley collection. Diameter 4.7 cm; 1944.Oc.1804. BOTTOM LEFT Diameter 11 cm; 1928.11-12.22. BOTTOM RIGHT Diameter 7.7 cm; 1928.11-12.25. BOTTOM CENTRE Diameter 9 cm; 1928.11-12.24.

Melanesia – Papua New Guinea – New Britain

76 LEFT Wooden shield painted black, red, blue and white with rattan (plant fibre) woven across it to form part of the pattern. Length 163 cm; 1913.5-24.15. CENTRE Carved shield, painted red, white and blue with rattan weaving. Length 135 cm; 1912-129. RIGHT Wooden shield made from three pieces and painted red, black and white. Length 133 cm; 1913.5-24.15.

Melanesia – Solomon Islands and Bougainville

The Solomon Islands stretch over 1400 km in a double chain of islands. There is no single 'Solomon Islands style' of art; the style of the Santa Cruz Islands in the far east of the group, for example, is quite different from that of other islands. There are, however, similarities, such as the wide use of animal motifs including the hornbill, frigate bird, shark, dolphin, pig, dog and snake. Shell is often used as a material for inlay in wood, or as an ornament in itself. Turtle-shell is another popular material used to great effect by the Solomon Islanders. Although Bougainville is now administered from Port Moresby in Papua New Guinea, it was considered to be part of the Solomon Islands at the time when many of these objects were collected and it has therefore been included in this group.

77 TOP LEFT Turtle-shell nose ornament in the shape of a human figure. Length 8 cm; 1908.6-24.59. TOP CENTRE Turtle-shell nose ornament. Length 7.5 cm; 7824. TOP RIGHT Turtle-shell nose ornament. Length 8.5 cm; Q72.Oc.75. CENTRE LEFT Ear plug of blackened wood, inlaid with pearl-shell. These ornaments and plainer wooden plugs, once common in Melanesia, are inserted into a hole made through the ear lobe (see **83**). Diameter 7 cm; 9142. CENTRE RIGHT Shell disc with incised and partly blackened pattern, from Bougainville. Diameter 11.3 cm; 1944.Oc.1394. BOTTOM LEFT Turtle-shell nose ornament collected in the late nineteenth century. Length 6.8 cm; 7825. BOTTOM RIGHT Turtle-shell nose ornament. Length 6.5 cm; 7826a.

78 TOP LEFT Breast ornament made from shell with turtle-shell overlay, from Bougainville. The hard and highly valued giant clam was once used for adze blades before the introduction of metal. Diameter 4.5 cm; 1944.Oc.2.1655. TOP CENTRE 'Chief's' breast ornament. In the Solomon Islands, as in other parts of Melanesia, leadership was seldom hereditary: village leaders attained their position through their deeds in life. The term 'chief' was often used by Europeans earlier this century. 'Head man' or 'big man' are more commonly used today. Length 20 cm; 1944.Oc.2.1337. TOP RIGHT Shell disc from Bougainville. Diameter 4.5 cm; 1944.Oc.2.1656. CENTRE Chief's breast ornament. Length 21.5 cm; +1159. BOTTOM LEFT Giant clam shell disc with turtle-shell overlay, from Bougainville. Diameter 4.75 cm; 1944.Oc.2.1670. BOTTOM CENTRE Breast ornament of giant clam shell with turtle-shell overlay, from Bougainville. Diameter 7 cm; 1944.Oc.2.1672. BOTTOM RIGHT Breast ornament from Bougainville. Diameter 7 cm; 1944.Oc.2.1678.

79 *Kapkap*. The form and manufacture of *kapkap* is similar throughout Melanesia (see **72**). In the Solomon Islands they were commonly worn on the forehead. TOP LEFT From Bougainville. Diameter 12 cm; 1944.Oc.2.1662. TOP RIGHT Diameter 12.8 cm; Q72.Oc.61. BOTTOM *Kapkap* from Malaita. Diameter 14.5 cm; 1944.Oc.2.1341.

80 Bamboo lime containers with burnt-on designs. In this method of ornamentation, which could also be described as incising, a hot, sharp point is used to mark designs on the surface of the bamboo, leaving blackish incision marks against the golden colour of the dried bamboo. TOP LEFT and TOP RIGHT Length 19 cm; 1957.Oc.4.10. TOP CENTRE Length 14.5 cm; 6422. BOTTOM From Buin Haku, Bougainville. Length 15.5 cm; 1944.Oc.2.1647.

81 Bamboo lime containers with incised designs. Large bamboo canes make ideal containers, as each hollow stem has natural divisions or chambers which can be left in or burnt out, depending upon the desired length of the container. TOP LEFT Length 16.7 cm; 6420. TOP RIGHT Length 16 cm; 1947.Oc.1.3. BOTTOM From San Cristoval. Length 34 cm; +4898.

82 This page of drawings shows some of the diversity in design found across the Solomon Islands. TOP LEFT From Santa Ana. Length 58 cm; 1937.4-15.5. TOP RIGHT From Russell Island. Length 50 cm; 1906.7-20.4. BOTTOM LEFT Length 27 cm; 1959.Oc.6.23. BOTTOM RIGHT Height 55 cm; 1937.4-15.5.

83 Canoe ornaments, carved from wood with shell inlay ornamentation and painted decoration. The shell decoration on these objects parallels tattoo patterns and shell-inlaid ear plugs (see **77**). Canoe prow ornaments shaped like human heads were fixed to canoe prows just above the water-line in order to guide the canoe through reefs, give protection to the warriors and ensure their success in battle (Chick 1978). TOP LEFT Height 24.5 cm; 1927-113. TOP RIGHT This bird-shaped fishing float was given to the Revd Hopkins in 1905. Such floats were made for special occasions and used only once. From north-eastern Malaita. Length 58 cm; 1944.Oc.2.1332. CENTRE Bird ornament from the south-eastern Solomon Islands. Length 23 cm; 1940.Oc.3.5. BOTTOM LEFT From the south-eastern Solomon Islands. Height 41 cm; 1947.Oc.12.3. BOTTOM RIGHT Height 31 cm; 1947.Oc.8.1.

84 TOP LEFT From Ulawa or Mala. Length 55 cm; 1940.Oc.3.21. TOP RIGHT From the south-eastern Solomon Islands. Diameter 21.5 cm; 1940.Oc.3.3. CENTRE LEFT From Malaita or Ulawa. Length 49 cm;

1940.Oc.3.20. BOTTOM From Ugi Island. Length 51.5 cm; 6355.

85 These shields are made of wickerwork over which resin has been added to form a flat surface. Red and black paint and elaborate shell inlay decorate the surface. These nineteenth-century shields were probably made for ceremonial use, although there is no documentation of their purpose in contemporary sources (Waite 1987). Only around twenty of these shields exist in museum collections and they are no longer made. LEFT Red and black painted wicker shield with white shell inlay. Length 87 cm; 1954.Oc.6.197. RIGHT Red and black painted wooden shield with white shell inlay. Length 75 cm; 8016.

86 TOP LEFT Carved wooden dance stick painted red and black, from northern Malaita. Length 44 cm; 1944.Oc.2.1334. TOP RIGHT Carved bird from a dance stick, painted red, black and white. Length 27 cm; 1904.6-21.15. BOTTOM LEFT Carved bone in the form of a shark-man, painted in a brownish red tone, from the south-eastern Solomon Islands. Length 41.5 cm; 1940.Oc.3.18. CENTRE RIGHT Carved wooden double-headed bird with red paint. Length 37 cm; 7905. BOTTOM Carved wooden bowl in the shape of a pig. Length 74 cm; +4978.

87 LEFT Wooden paddle with black painted design. Designs are outlined with a sharp point and the surrounding wood is then cut away. Length 161 cm; 1912.7-8.2. CENTRE Wooden dance club painted black and yellow. Length 138 cm; 1927-92. RIGHT Wooden paddle with black painted design of frigate birds fishing. Length 146 cm; 1950.Oc.4.6.

88 Turtle-shell and pearl-shell pendants. These abstract designs incorporate the typical Solomon Islands motifs of the frigate bird and fish. TOP LEFT Shell pendant. Length 6 cm; 1944.Oc.2.1363. TOP RIGHT Shell pendant. Length 9.5 cm; 1959.Oc.6.6. CENTRE LEFT Turtle-shell pendant from a glass bead necklace (not illustrated). Length 9 cm; +3890. CENTRE Shell pendant. Length 11 cm; 1944.Oc.21.1781. CENTRE RIGHT Shell pendant. Length 5.5 cm; 1959.Oc.6.5. BOTTOM LEFT Diameter 7.2 cm; 1944.Oc.2.1780. BOTTOM CENTRE Nose ornament of shell. Width 11 cm; 1944.Oc.2.1234. BOTTOM RIGHT Shell pendant. Length 8.5 cm; 1959.Oc.6.7.

89 LEFT Engraved wooden club from Shortland Island. Length 116 cm; 1929.7-13.90. CENTRE Engraved wooden club. Length 100 cm; 1900-65. RIGHT Engraved wooden club. Length 90 cm; 1949.Oc.5.1.

Melanesia – Solomon Islands – Santa Cruz Islands

The curve is the predominant design feature in the art of the eastern Solomon Islands. The curve of the bowls, dance sticks and other implements recalls that of the canoe. Santa Cruz *kapkap* were worn as neck pendants: typically a large area of white shell was exposed and ornamented with stylised designs in turtle-shell, such as frigate birds with long forked tails and outstretched wings and repeated double-fish motifs.

90 *Tema (kapkap)*, shell discs with turtle-shell overlay. TOP LEFT Diameter 12.5 cm; 1944.Oc.2.1192. TOP CENTRE Diameter 16.5 cm; 1944.Oc.2.1191. TOP RIGHT Diameter 10 cm; 1913.11-15.46. CENTRE LEFT Diameter 11.5 cm; 1929.3-4.6. CENTRE Diameter 13.5 cm; 1944.Oc.2.1187. CENTRE RIGHT Diameter 13 cm; 1944.Oc.2.1186. BOTTOM LEFT Diameter 11.5 cm; 1944.Oc.2.1189. BOTTOM RIGHT Diameter 14 cm; 1944.Oc.2.1185.

91 Red and black painted dance staffs. These staffs were designed for use in the *napa* dance at children's initiation feasts (Waite 1983). LEFT Length 84 cm; 1929.7-13.91. CENTRE LEFT Length 88 cm; 1921.11-2.46. CENTRE RIGHT Length 88 cm; 1980.Oc.1.2. RIGHT Length 66.5 cm; 95.12-18.1.

92 Decorated gourd containers with burnt-on designs. TOP LEFT Length 24.5 cm; 1954.Oc.6.204. TOP RIGHT Length 24 cm; +4914. BOTTOM LEFT Length 17.5 cm; 1944.Oc.2.1200b. BOTTOM RIGHT Length 14.2 cm; 1956.Oc.6.206.

93 Painted wooden bowls or scoops, from the Beasley collection. TOP LEFT and BOTTOM RIGHT Side and underneath of a scoop. Length 39.5 cm; 1944.Oc.2.1197. MIDDLE LEFT and RIGHT Side and underneath of a bowl. Length 31 cm; 1929.3-4.21.

Melanesia – Vanuatu – Banks Islands

94 Plaited palm-leaf headbands with anthropomorphic figure pattern. Lengths 64-98 cm; 1944.Oc.2.1086-96.

95 Fine plaited-leaf mats from Vanuatu are some-times worn by women at dances. These dance mats are said to have been worn for the *qat* dance. TOP Length 102 cm; 1905.5-17.6. CENTRE Length 108 cm; 1905.2-17.5. BOTTOM Length 106 cm; 1931.7-22.75.

Melanesia – New Caledonia

96 Scenes from a 'chief's' staff (see **97**), perhaps illustrating a mythical or historical event. Length 112 cm; 1913.11-15.369.

97 Scenes from a 'chief's' staff (see **96**), perhaps illustrating a mythical or historical event. Length 120 cm; 1954.Oc.6.

98 Wooden carvings from New Caledonia. LEFT Carved wooden house board with red painted details. The squat, broad-nosed face of the figure is typical of the style of the French territory of New Caledonia (see **99** and **100**). Length 45 cm; 1913.11-15.359. CENTRE Carved wooden club. Length 67.5 cm; 1957.Oc.11.1. RIGHT Carved wooden face with frog and fish. Length 22 cm; 98.7-4.49.

99 New Caledonian houses were once round and thatched, with convex wooden door jambs. The roof finial stood upright, surmounting the conical thatch (Moore 1995). LEFT Carved wooden house board. Height 173 cm; 1941.Oc.1.7. CENTRE Wooden roof finial. Height 173 cm; 1925.7-11.1. RIGHT Carved wooden house board. Height 165 cm; 1962.Oc.3.3.

100 Masks originally formed part of costumes. TOP LEFT and TOP RIGHT Two views of a carved wooden face. Height 40.5 cm; 1913.11-15.358. BOTTOM LEFT Carved wooden face. Height 49 cm; 1955.Oc.6.257. BOTTOM RIGHT Carved wooden figure from the end of a staff, showing how a mask may have looked when complete, with attachments of human hair on the head and beard and the dramatic sweep of dark feathers cascading over the shoulders. Length of whole staff 69 cm; 1913.11-15.361.

Further Reading

Beck, R. and Neich, R., 'Jades of the New Zealand Maori', in S. Markel, *From The World of Jade*, Marg Publications, Bombay, 1992

Buck, P. (Te Rangi Hiroa), *Arts and Crafts of Hawaii*, Bishop Museum Press, Honolulu, 1957

Bunge, F. and Cooke, M. (eds), *Oceania: A Regional Study*, US Government Printing Office, Washington, DC, 1985

Caruana, W., *Aboriginal Art*, Thames and Hudson, London, 1993

Chick, J. and S. (eds), *Grass Roots Art of the Solomons: Images and Islands*, Pacific Publications, Sydney, 1978

Coote, J. and Shelton, A. (eds), *Anthropology, Art and Aesthetics*, Clarendon Press, Oxford, 1992

Dark, P. and Rose, R., *Artistic Heritage in a Changing Pacific*, University of Hawaii Press, Honolulu, 1993

Ewins, R., *Fijian Artefacts*, Tasmanian Museum and Art Gallery, Hobart, 1982

Kaeppler, A., *Artificial Curiosities: An Exposition of Native Manufactures Collected on the Three Pacific Voyages of Captain James Cook, R.N.*, Bishop Museum Press, Honolulu, 1978

Lincoln, L., *Assemblage of Spirits: Idea and Image in New Ireland*, George Braziller and Minneapolis Institute of Arts, New York, 1987

Mead, S. M., *Material Culture and Art in the Star Harbour Region, Eastern Solomon Islands*, Royal Ontario Museum, Toronto, 1973

Newton, D., *Art Styles of the Papuan Gulf*, Museum of Primitive Art, New York, 1961

O'Hanlon, M., *Paradise: Portraying the New Guinea Highlands*, British Museum Press, London, 1993

Phelps, S., *Art and Artefacts of the Pacific, Africa and the Americas: The James Hooper Collection*, Hutchinson, London, 1975

Simmons, D., *Art of the Pacific*, Oxford University Press, Wellington, NZ, 1979

Starzecka, D. C. (ed.), *Maori Art and Culture*, British Museum Press, London, 1996, rev. 1998

Taylor, P., Aragon, L. and Rice, A., *Beyond the Java Sea: Art of Indonesia's Outer Islands*, Smithsonian Institution Press, Washington, DC, 1991

Thomas, N., *Oceanic Art*, Thames and Hudson, London, 1995

Van Tilburg, J. A., *Easter Island: Archaeology, Ecology and Culture*, British Museum Press, London, 1994

Waite, D., *Art of the Solomon Islands from the Collection of the Barber-Müller Museum*, Geneva, 1983

Waite, D., *Artefacts from the Solomon Islands in the Julius L. Benchley Collection*, British Museum Publications, London, 1987

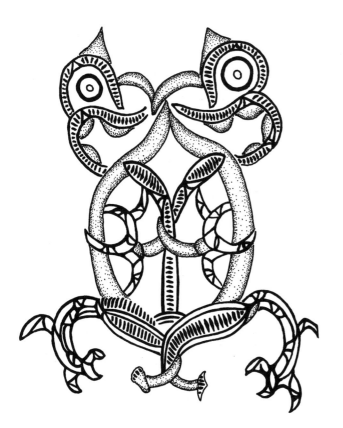

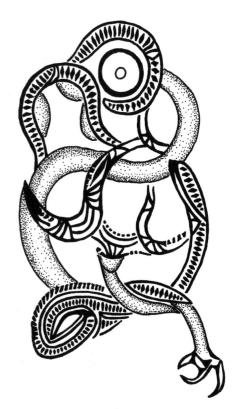

1 Carved designs from wooden Maori *hoe* (paddles) from New Zealand.

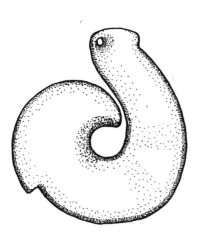
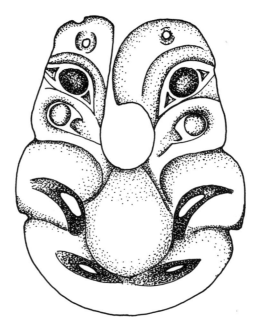

2 Maori pendants of bone and nephrite, from New Zealand. TOP LEFT and RIGHT *hei tiki*, pendants (*hei*) representing the human form (*tiki*); BOTTOM LEFT *hei matau* or fish-hook pendant; BOTTOM CENTRE a unique *hei tiki*; BOTTOM RIGHT *koropepe*, a representation of a coiled eel-like animal.

3 Maori wood carvings from New Zealand. TOP CENTRE carved in the 1990s, shows a European holding a quill; RIGHT Maori ancestor figure holding a club, carved in the mid-nineteenth century; BOTTOM spirals carved on a canoe prow.

4 *Tata*, Maori canoe bailers carved from wood, from New Zealand.

5 TOP and CENTRE Details from two Maori *hoe* (paddles); BOTTOM a face carved on a
wooden flute; all from New Zealand.

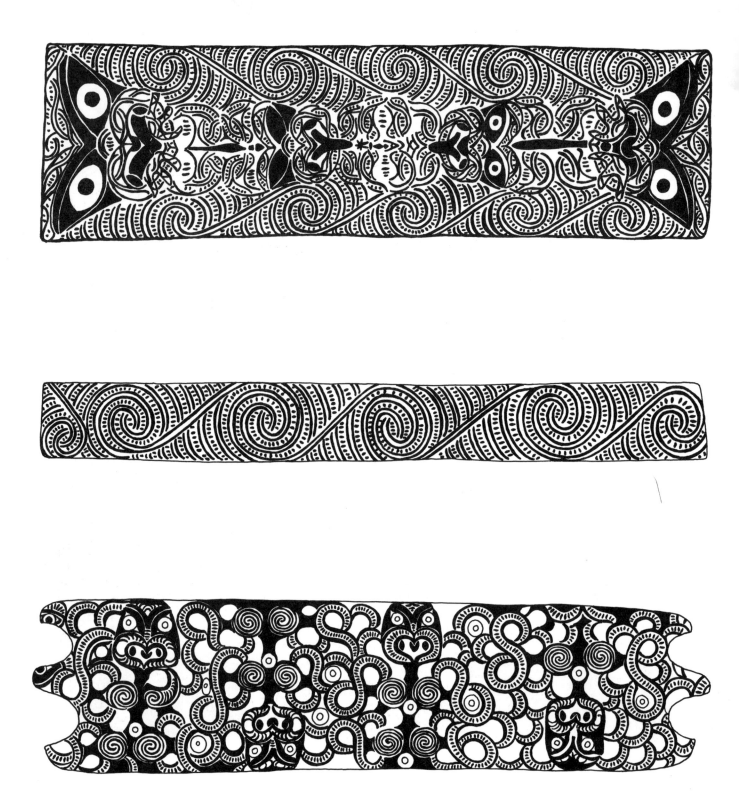

6 *Wakahuia* (Maori treasure boxes) from New Zealand. *Wakahuia* were richly carved on all sides, as they were hung from the rafters for storage.

7 Lids of *wakahuia* (treasure boxes) from New Zealand.

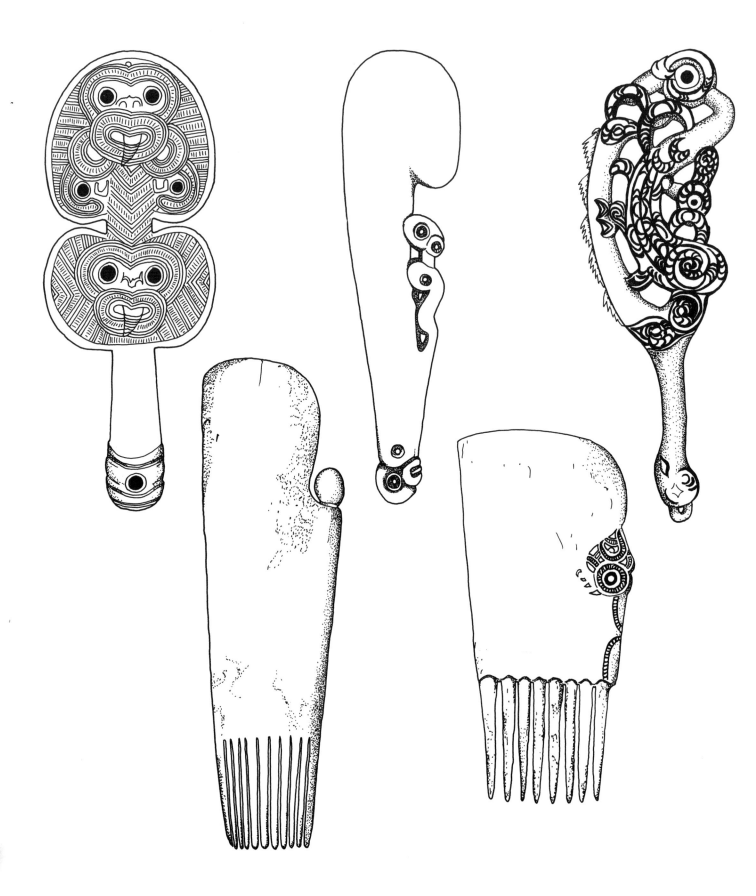

8 TOP ROW Maori weapons, including TOP RIGHT a knife edged in sharks' teeth; BOTTOM two whalebone *heru* (combs) worn in the hair as ornaments; all from New Zealand.

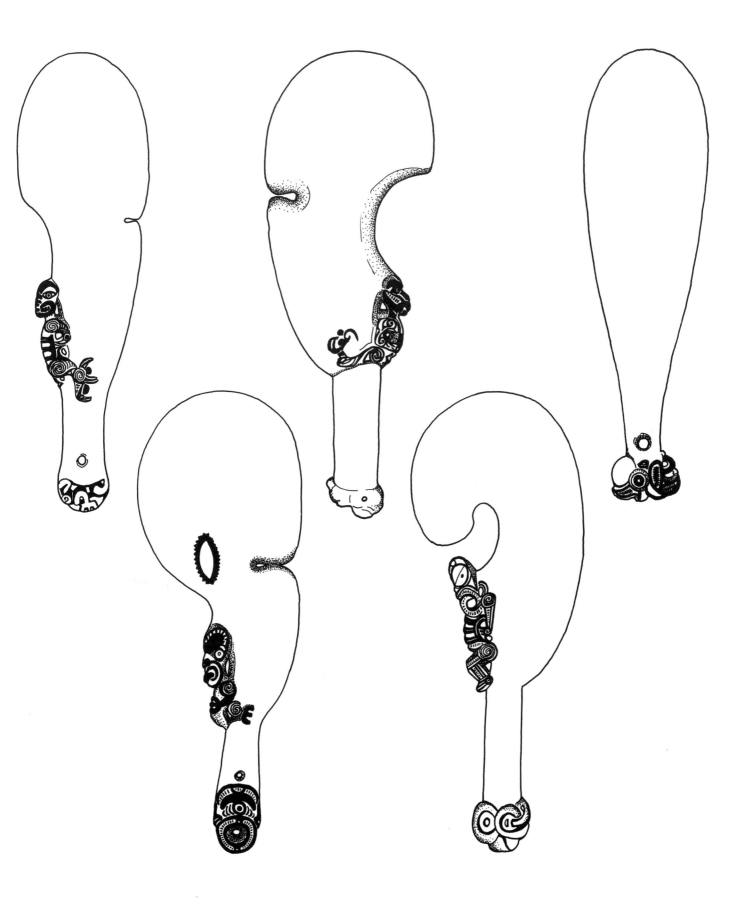

9 Maori *wahaika* and *mere*, types of wood or bone club, from New Zealand.

10 *Patu* and *mere*, types of Maori club, made of wood or bone. BOTTOM RIGHT a *kotiate* club, which literally means 'cut liver'.

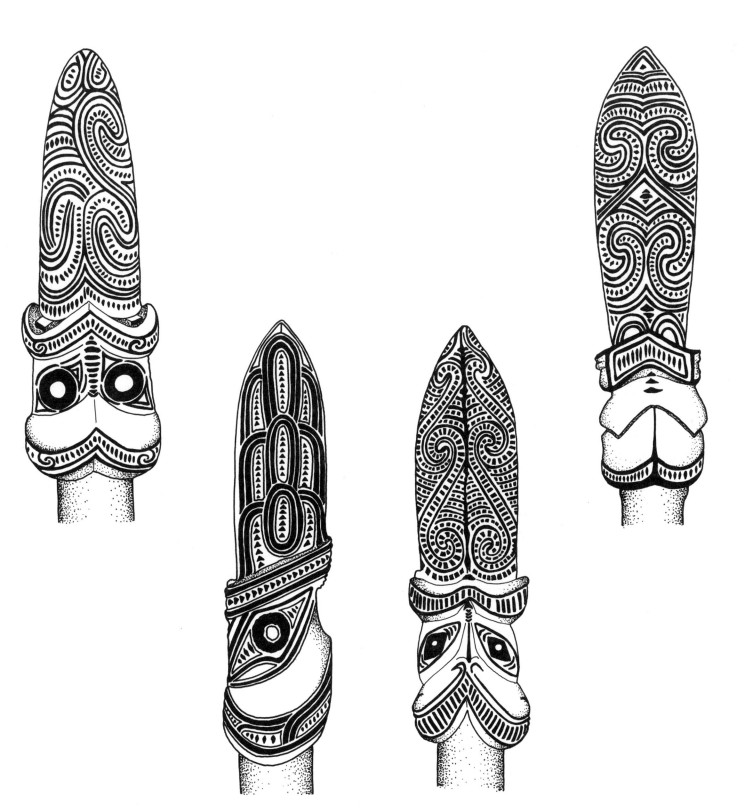

11 *Taiaha*, a type of Maori quarterstaff, from New Zealand. The design shows
a head with projecting tongue, which can be seen clearly when the drawing is viewed
upside down.

12 Recent Maori art from New Zealand. The circular designs are from a ball made of pottery, a new material in Maori art. The pendant BOTTOM LEFT is in the form of a flying bat; BOTTOM RIGHT is a pendant named *paikea*, meaning 'whale'.

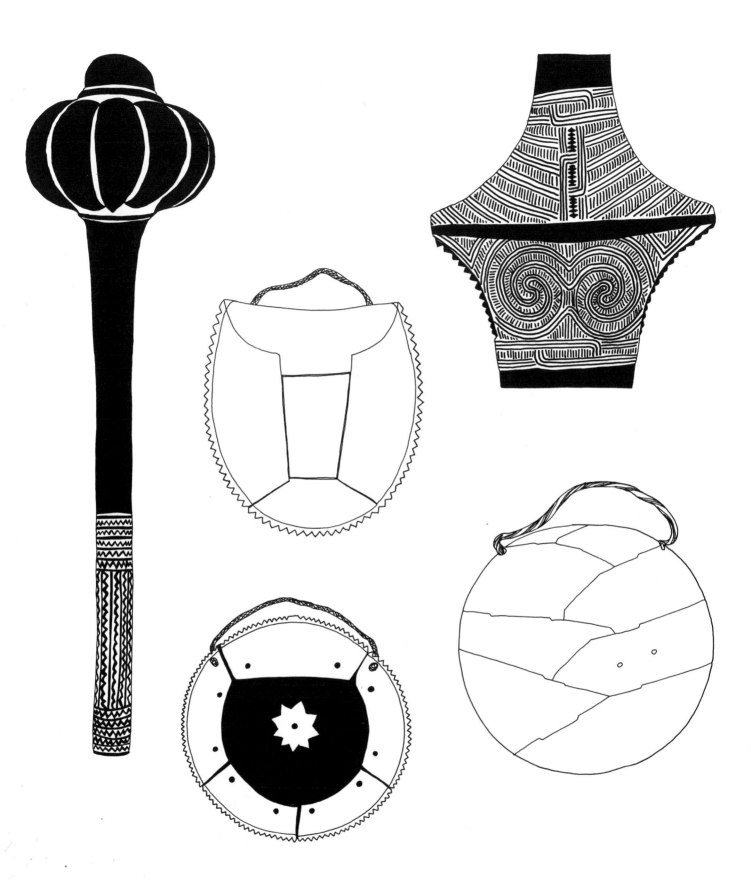

13 Artefacts from Fiji. LEFT wooden club; TOP RIGHT detail of the carved decoration on
a club; CENTRE and BOTTOM three breast ornaments made of whalebone sections finely
pieced together. Such items were owned only by those of high rank.

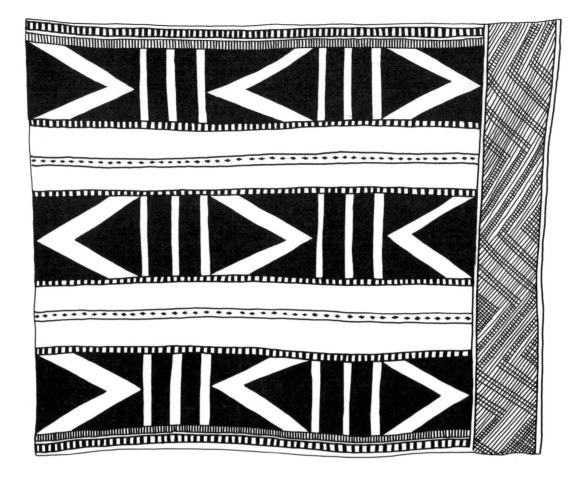

14 Barkcloth designs from Fiji.

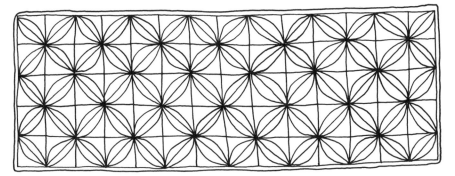
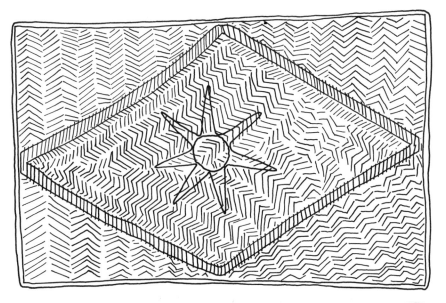

15 *Kupeti* (tablets for printing barkcloth designs) from Fiji. The tablets were made from leaf or wood with coconut fibre midribs sewn over to make a raised pattern.

16 Details of two barkcloths from Wallis and Futuna.

17 Details of two barkcloth designs from Wallis and Futuna.

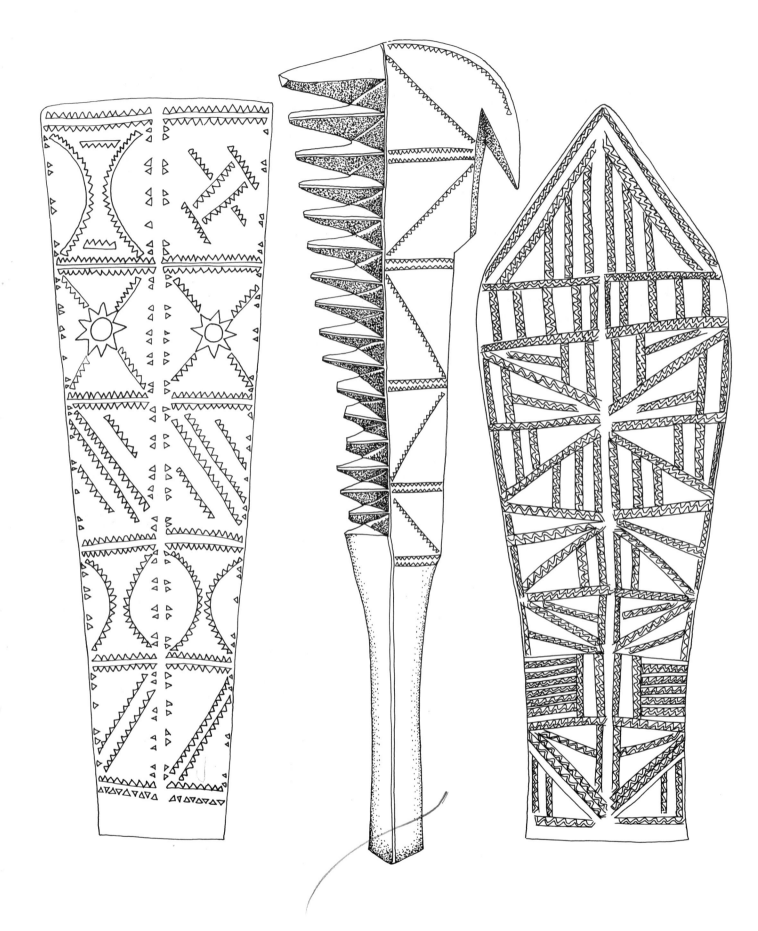

18 Samoan wooden clubs.

19 Barkcloth from Samoa.

20 Section of a painted Niue barkcloth.

21 Painted barkcloth from Niue. Floral motifs such as these appealed to the aesthetic taste of Europeans who visited the islands in the eighteenth and nineteenth centuries.

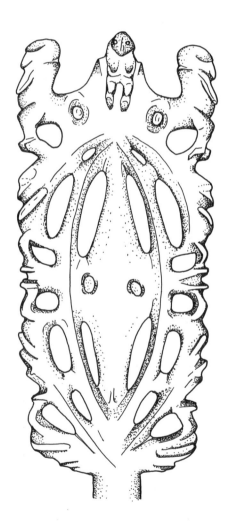

22 Rarotongan carving and Cook Islands work can either be obviously anthropomorphic, as the rare figure TOP LEFT and RIGHT shows, or abstract, as can be seen in the repetition of form at the sides of the BOTTOM figure, a 'godstick'. Missionaries discouraged the use of such figures, which they considered 'idolatrous'.

23 Details from handles of Cook Islands ceremonial adzes.

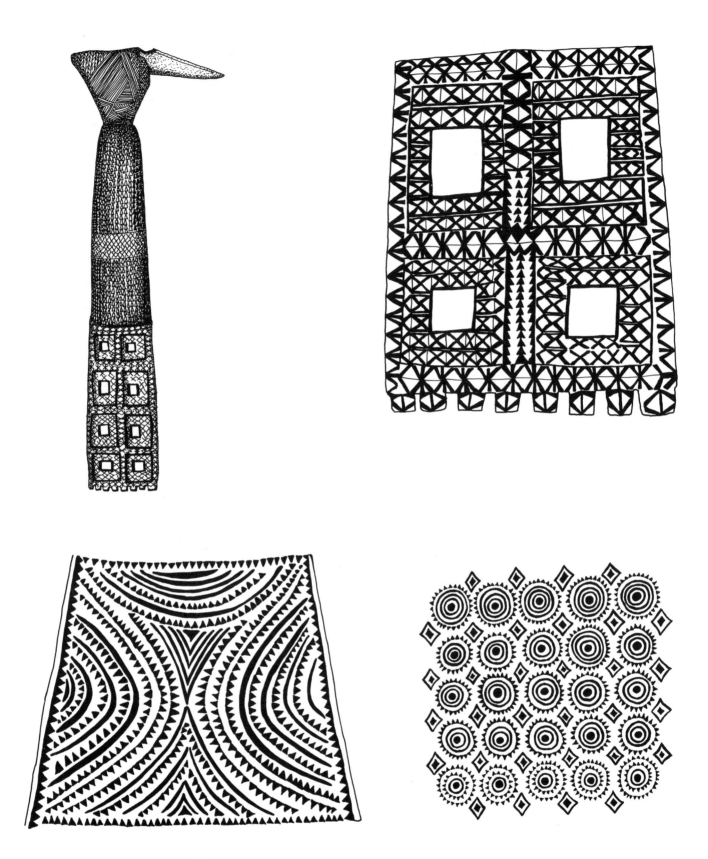

24 TOP Ceremonial adze from the Cook Islands, with detail; BOTTOM designs from ceremonial paddles and adzes from the Austral Islands.

25 Carved designs on ceremonial paddles and adzes from the Austral Islands.

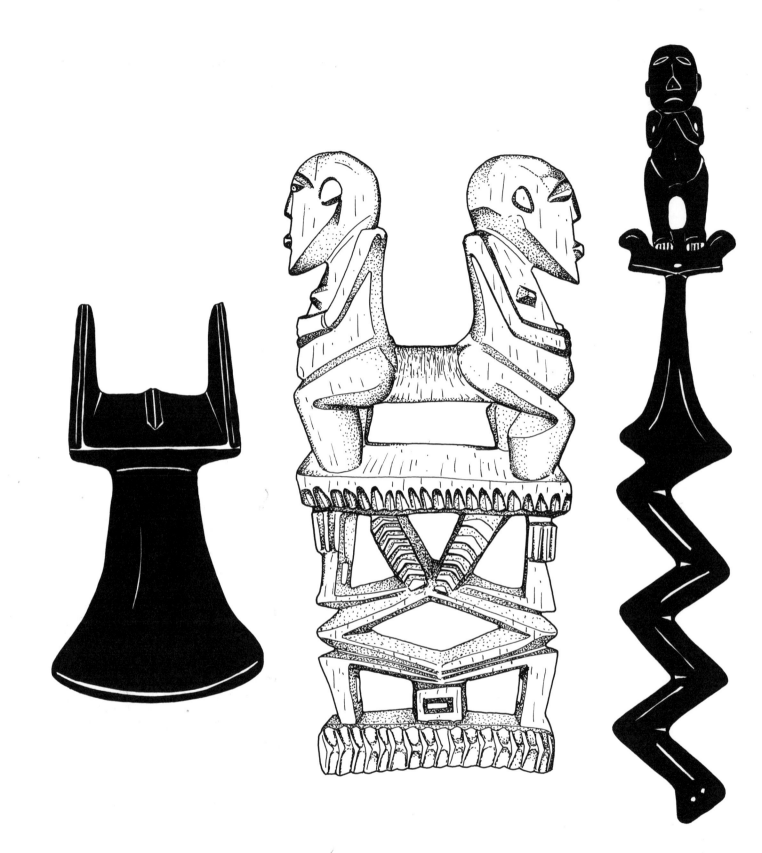

26 Artefacts from Tahiti, Society Islands. It is possible that the stone pounder LEFT was collected during one of Captain Cook's voyages. These pounders are a fine example of the beautiful form of utilitarian objects. CENTRE Carved wooden canoe ornament; RIGHT the handle of a wooden fly whisk.

27 Barkcloth decorated with leaf-print designs from Tahiti, Society Islands. The sparse leafy designs are typical of early Society Islands *tapa*.

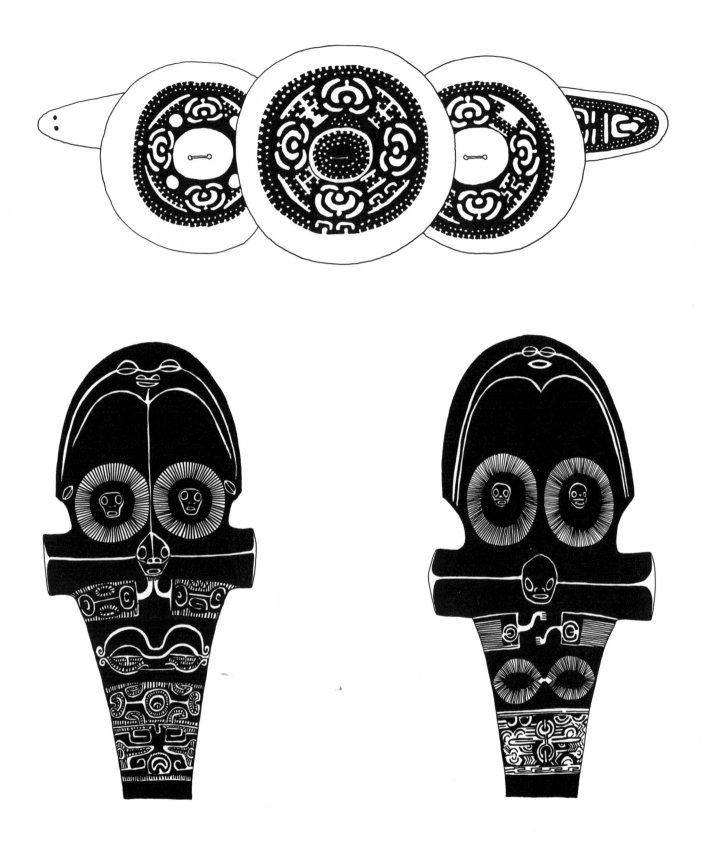

28 TOP Marquesas Islands pearl-shell headband with turtle-shell overlay;
BOTTOM detail of a club showing the Marquesas style of carving face designs with
smaller face and eye patterns within them. Such specialised weapons were probably
carved by the *tuhuna*, highly ranked artisans.

29 Carved wooden bowls from the Marquesas Islands. The patterns are similar to designs used in tattooing.

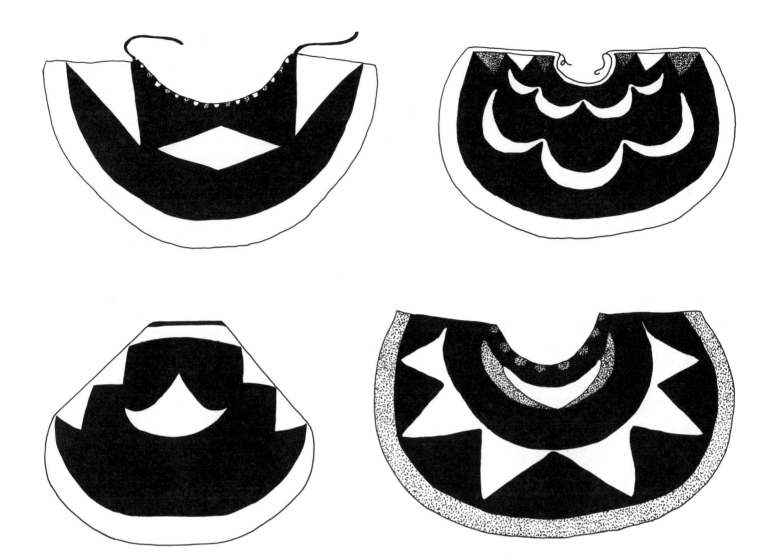
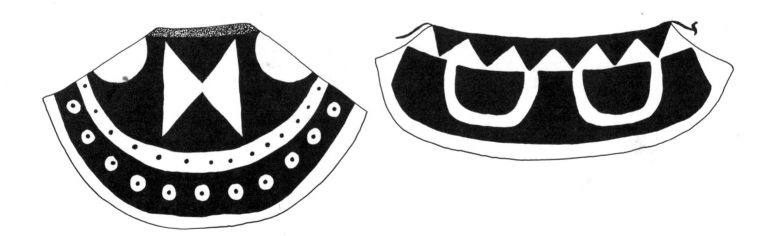

30 Designs of feather cloaks and capes from Hawaii. The main colours of these are bright yellow, red and black. Cloaks were worn both for protection in warfare and as a sign of rank.

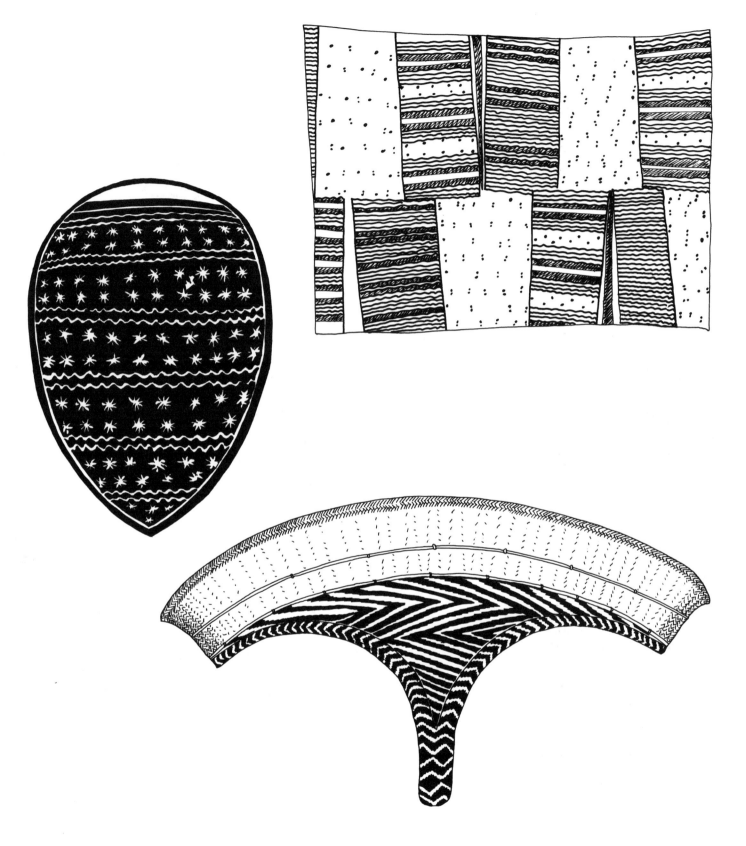

31 BOTTOM Fan; CENTRE LEFT detail of a pattern on a gourd; TOP RIGHT decorated barkcloth; all from Hawaii. Hawaiians used beaters to impress a 'watermark' pattern on the background cloth and bamboo stamps to create distinctive decorative patterns on the surface.

32 Artefacts from Easter Island. RIGHT anthropomorphic wooden dance paddle; CENTRE pattern on an ancestor figurine (**33**); TOP LEFT petroglyph with bird-man figure; BOTTOM LEFT detail from the butt of a wooden club. Wooden artefacts from Easter Island often have a highly polished sheen.

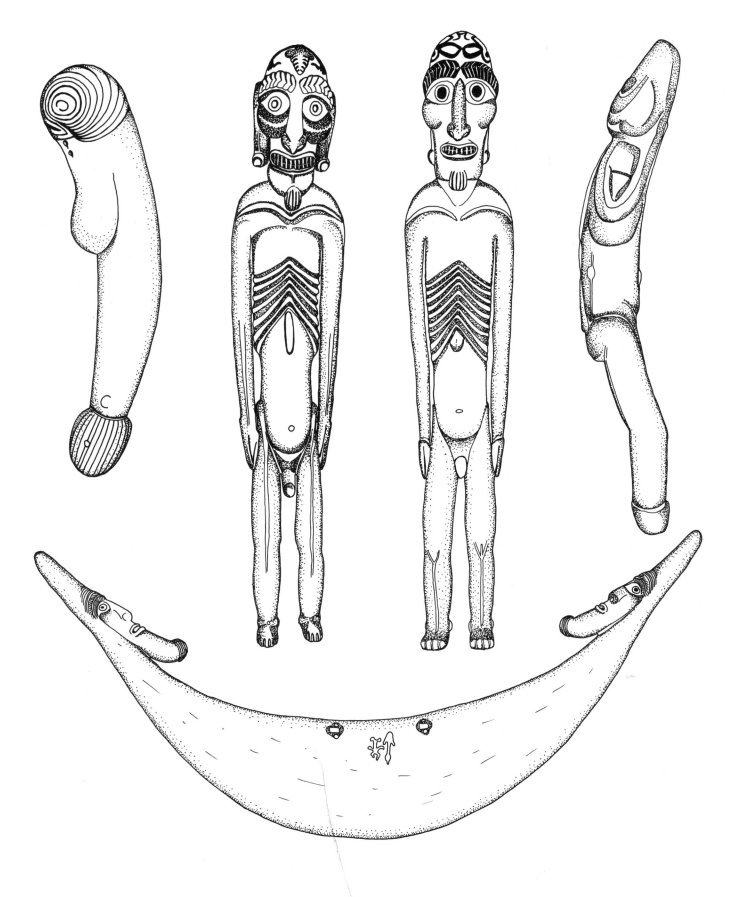

33 TOP Carved wooden figures from Easter Island; BOTTOM *rei miro* (breast ornament)
which evokes the shape of the new moon.

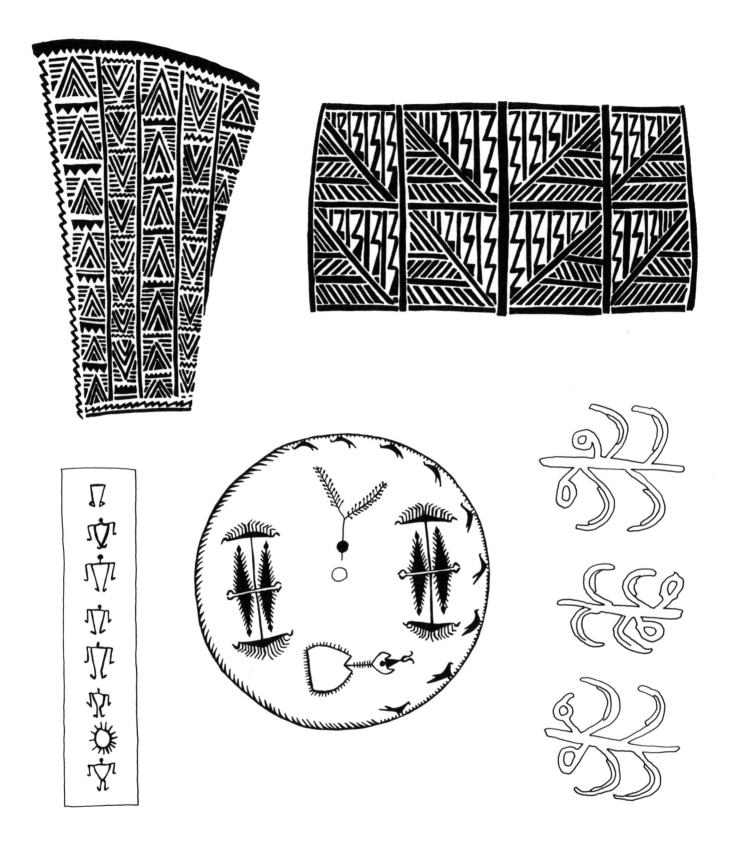

34 TOP Incised geometric designs from Tongan wooden clubs;
BOTTOM figures and patterns from Tongan artefacts.

35 Decorations from Marshall Islands plaited mats.

36 Carved wooden bowls with white shell inlay, from Belau, Micronesia.

37 Shell inlay decorations on wooden objects from Belau, Micronesia.
TOP RIGHT bowl; CENTRE sword; LEFT container for traditional money.

38 Wooden tablets from Pohnpei, Micronesia, carved with low-relief patterns illustrating some of the conventional woven textile designs of the islands.

39 Carved wooden pattern tablets from Pohnpei, Micronesia.

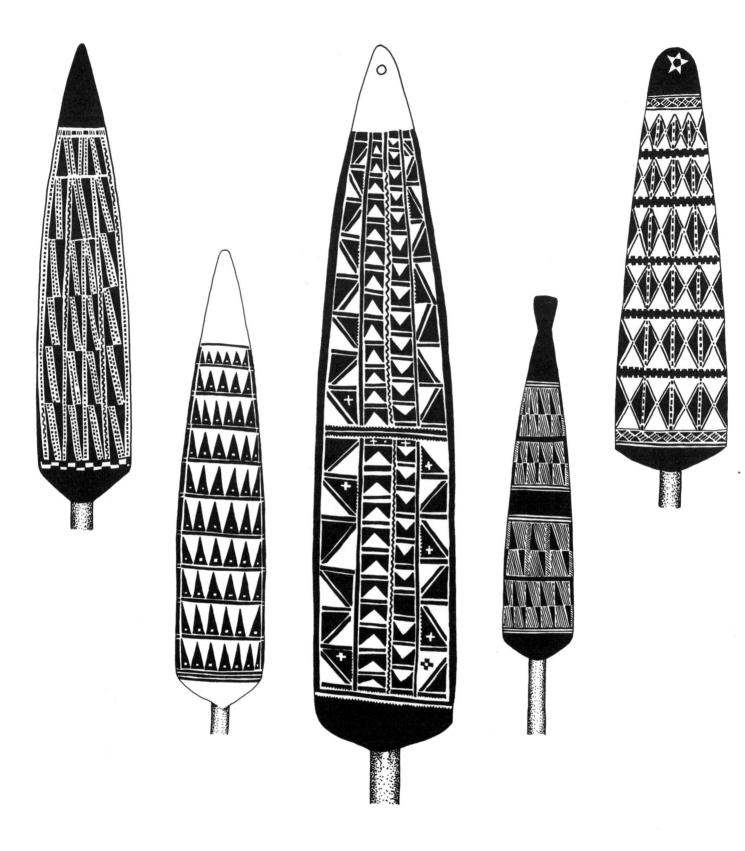

40 Decorated wooden dance paddles from the Mortlock Islands, Micronesia.

41 Engraved figures and animals on dried baobab nuts from Western Australia.

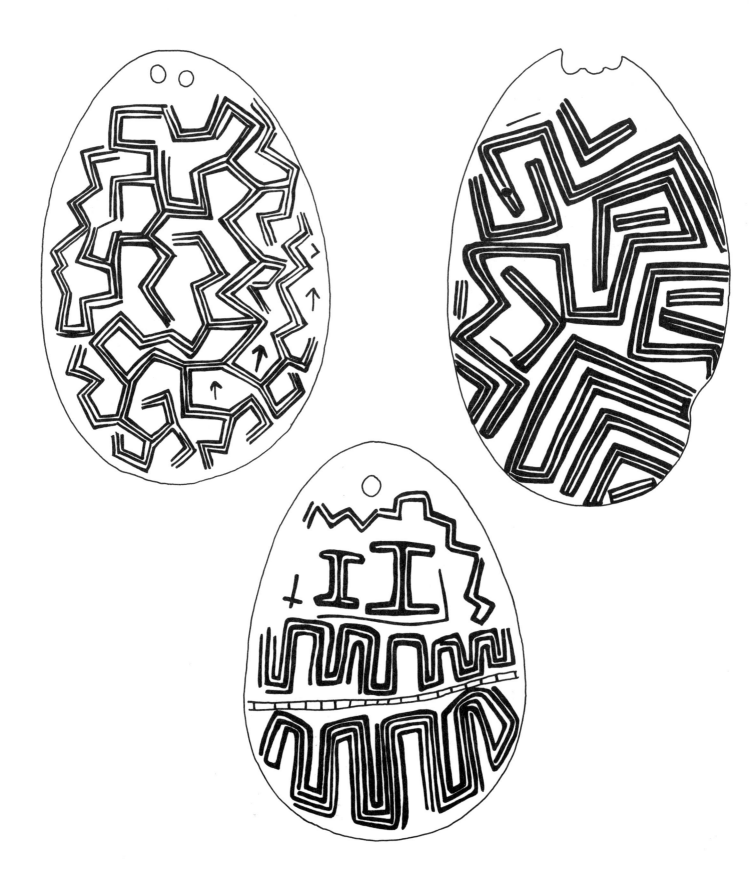

42 Engraved pearl-shell pubic covers from Western Australia.

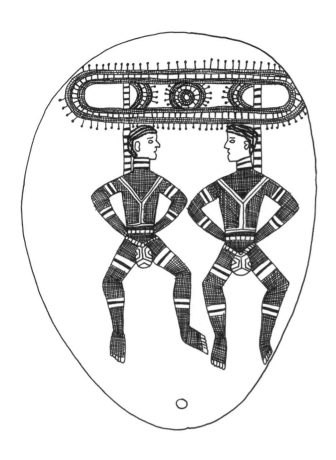

43 Engraved pearl-shell pubic covers from Western Australia.

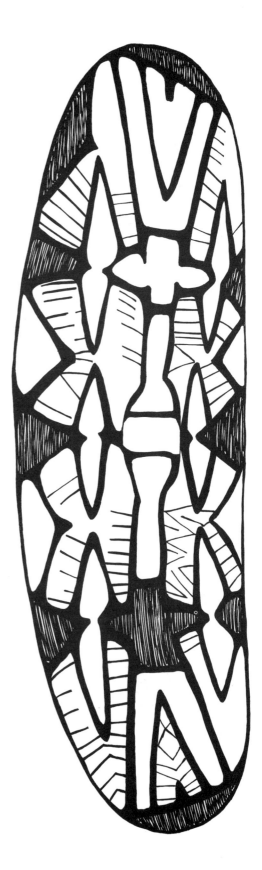

44 Wooden shields painted with red, white, yellow and black,
from Queensland, Australia.

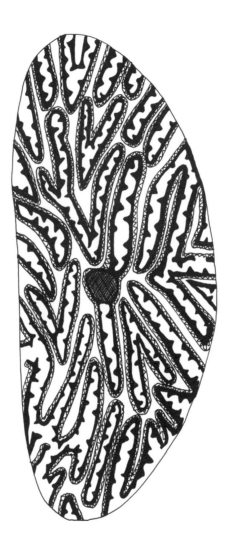

45 Painted wooden shields from Queensland, Australia.

46 Bark painting of a shark and magpie geese, from Ramingining, Arnhemland, Northern Territory, Australia. The bold, striking patterns of such work have proved popular on the international art market and on local tourist art objects, such as T-shirts.

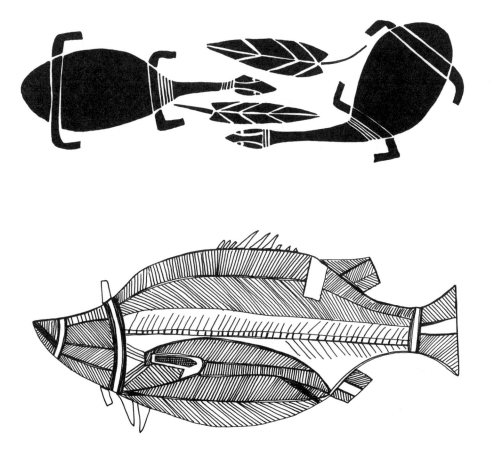

47 Bark painting showing kangaroos, long-necked tortoises and a fish, from Arnhemland, Northern Territory, Australia.

48 Torres Strait Islands objects of turtle-shell, collected by the anthropologist
A. C. Haddon in 1888.

49 TOP and BOTTOM Carved wooden headrests; CENTRE wooden canoe prow ornament;
all from Irian Jaya.

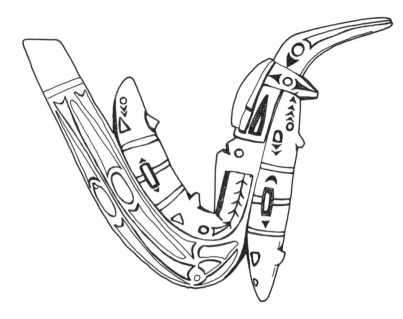
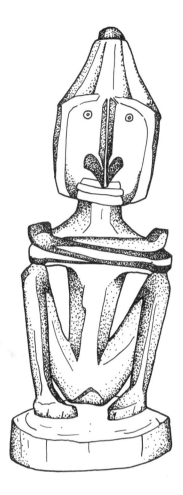

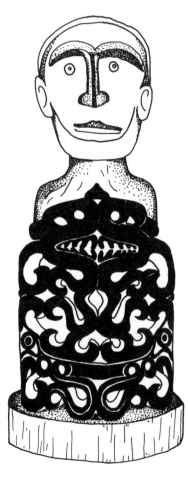

50 Objects from Irian Jaya. TOP LEFT carved wooden canoe prow ornament;
TOP RIGHT and BOTTOM RIGHT *korwar* (ancestor figure); BOTTOM LEFT shield used
for an ancestor figure.

51 Decorated containers of coconut shell from Madang and Tami Island,
Papua New Guinea.

52 *Bilum* (net-bags) made by the Wahgi people of the Western Highlands Province, Papua New Guinea. The patterns on these colourful bags incorporate new symbols and materials.

53 *Bilum* (net-bags) made by the Wahgi people of the Western Highlands Province, Papua New Guinea. TOP pattern called 'one ace', which reflects the local enthusiasm for card games. The designs BOTTOM LEFT (the cross) and BOTTOM RIGHT (angels) indicate the influence of missionaries in the region.

54 Painted wooden shields made by the Wahgi people of the Western Highlands Province, Papua New Guinea. The shield designs deploy non-traditional imagery to express local political tensions.

55 Painted wooden shields from West Sepik Province, Papua New Guinea.

56 Food hook and pottery bowl from East Sepik Province, Papua New Guinea.

57 Papua New Guinean designs from East Sepik Province.
TOP and BOTTOM LEFT pottery bowls; TOP RIGHT carved wooden headrest;
BOTTOM RIGHT painted wooden carving.

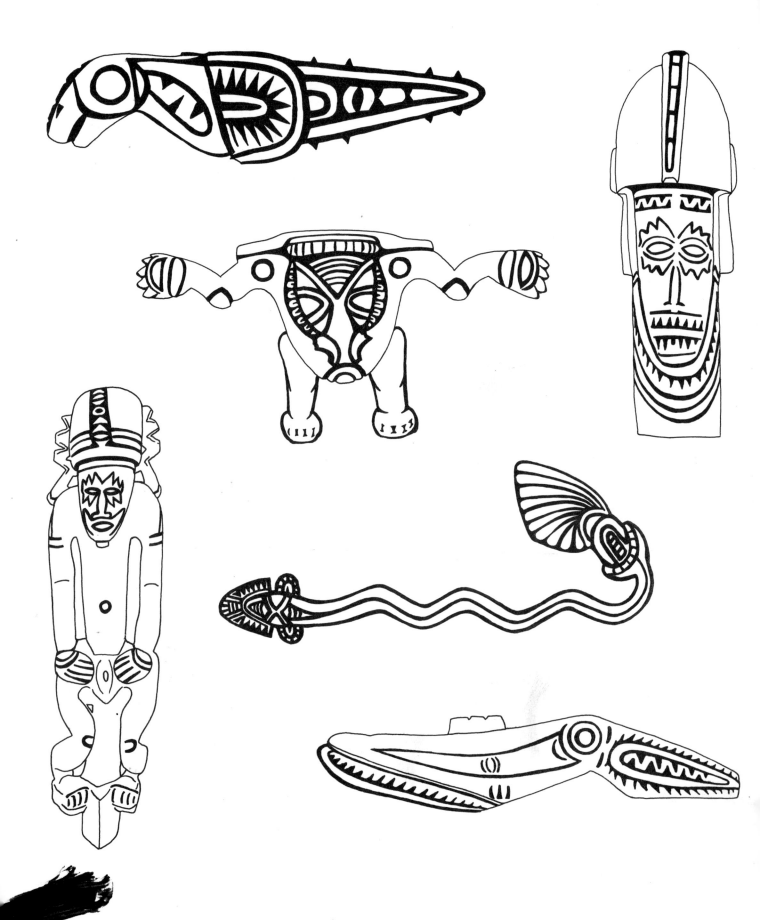

58 Incised, painted and carved designs on wooden bowls, figures and a staff from Tami Island, Huon Gulf, Papua New Guinea.

59 Decorations on wooden bowls and dishes from Tami Island, Huon Gulf, Papua New Guinea.

60 Carved and painted wooden headrests from Tami Island, Huon Gulf,
Papua New Guinea.

61 Carved and painted wooden headrests from Tami Island, Huon Gulf, Papua New Guinea.

62 Wooden carvings from the Milne Bay District and the Trobriand Islands, Papua New Guinea. CENTRE LEFT canoe splash-board, collected early this century by the celebrated anthropologist Branislaw Malinowski.

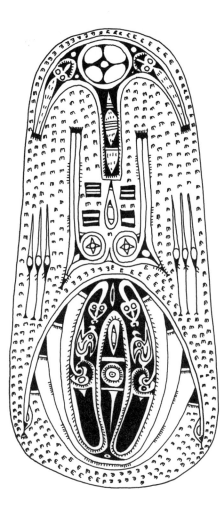

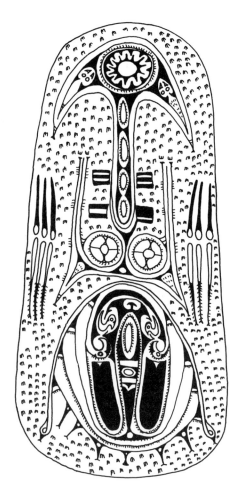

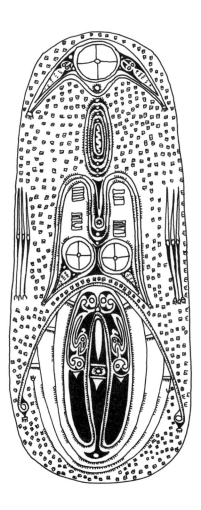

63 Black, red and white painted shields from the Trobriand Islands,
Papua New Guinea.

64 Decorated lime gourds from the Trobriand Islands, Papua New Guinea. The pattern is burned on to the surface with a hot point.

65 Engraved patterns on bowls and lime spatulas from the Trobriand Islands, Papua New Guinea. Lime is mixed with betel nut and chewed as a mild stimulant.

66 Decorations on carved wooden clubs with lime inlay, from the Milne Bay District and the Trobriand Islands, Papua New Guinea.

67 Decorated wooden lime spatulas and pestles from the Milne Bay District and the Trobriand Islands, Papua New Guinea.

68 LEFT and RIGHT Painted and engraved wooden bull-roarers; CENTRE BOTTOM shield;
TOP CENTRE ancestral shield; all from the Papuan Gulf, Papua New Guinea.

69 Painted and carved shields and ceremonial boards from the Papuan Gulf, Papua New Guinea. Wooden boards such as these are personal objects hung in men's houses.

70 Spoons carved from coconut shells with lime inlay, from the Papuan Gulf,
Papua New Guinea.

71 Carved wooden lime spatulas from Hermit Island, part of Manus Province,
Papua New Guinea. CENTRE LEFT two lizard-like shapes with curving tails;
LEFT and RIGHT spiral frets recall the spiral motif in the tail.

72 Discs of shell with turtle-shell overlay, called *kapkap* and worn by men, from Manus Province, Papua New Guinea.

73 Finely worked turtle-shell decoration from a Manus Province *kapkap*,
Papua New Guinea.

74 Painted wooden bird ornaments and a pattern from a friction gong,
from New Ireland Province, Papua New Guinea.

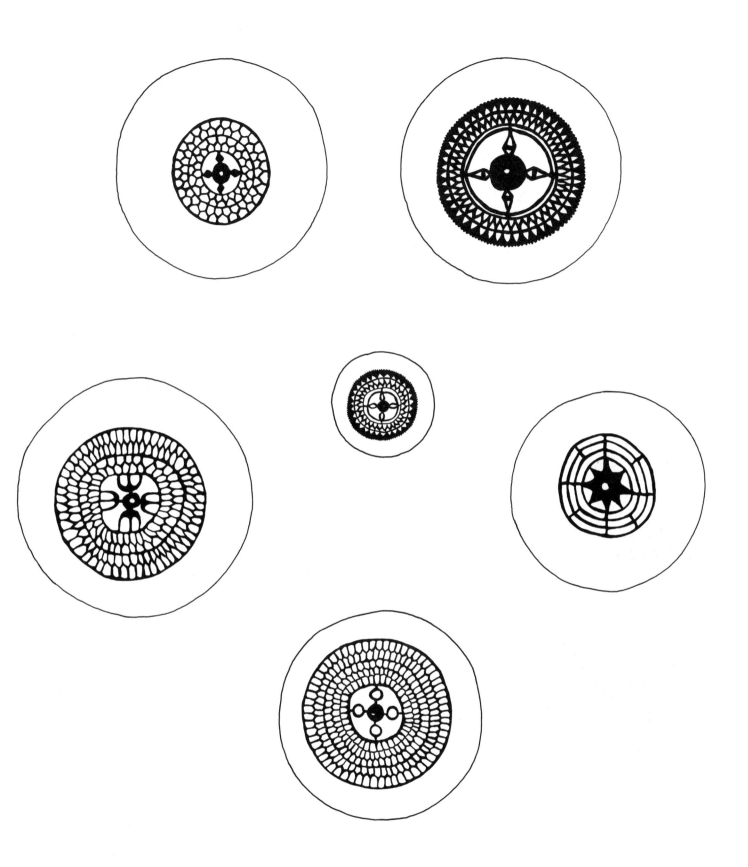

75 *Kapkap* (shell ornaments) from New Ireland Province, Papua New Guinea.

76 Three shields from New Britain, made of wood and vegetable fibre
with painted designs.

77 Turtle-shell nose ornaments, a shell disc from Bougainville and a wooden ear plug
from the Solomon Islands.

78 Breast ornaments from Bougainville and the Solomon Islands.

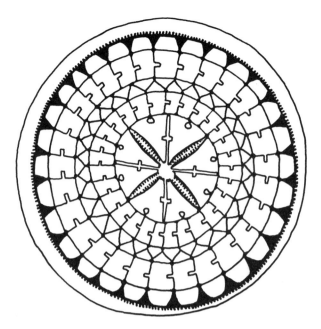

79 *Kapkap* (shell ornaments) from Bougainville and the Solomon Islands. The fine
workmanship of these turtle-shell and shell ornaments is an impressive testament to
the skill of the artists.

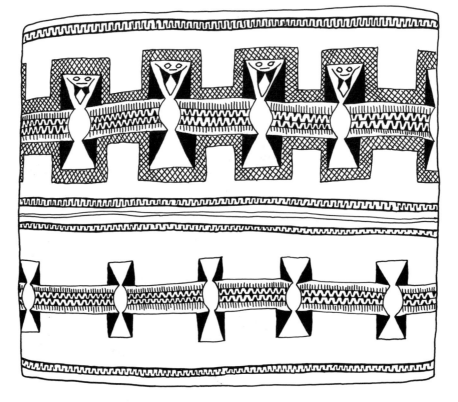

80 Incised bamboo lime containers from the Solomon Islands and Bougainville.
TOP CENTRE the frigate bird; others depict human figures and faces.

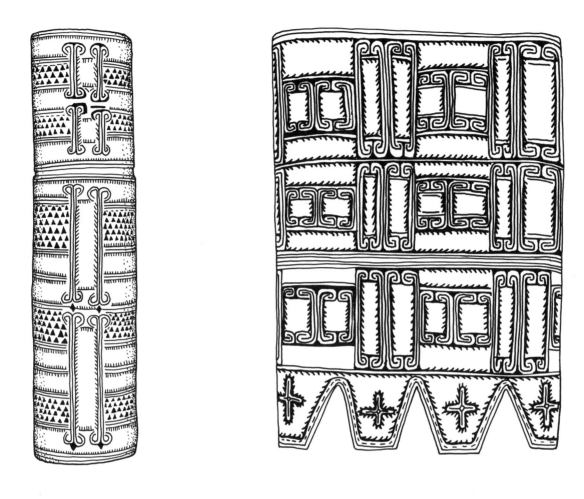

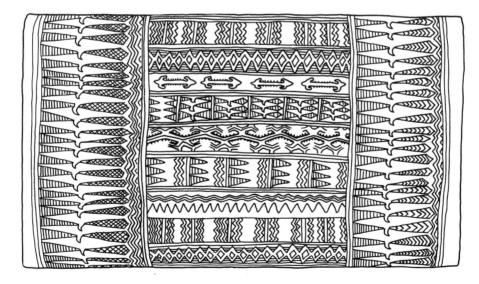

81 Bamboo lime boxes with incised patterns, from the Solomon Islands. Charcoal and sap are rubbed into the cuts to make a dark pattern.

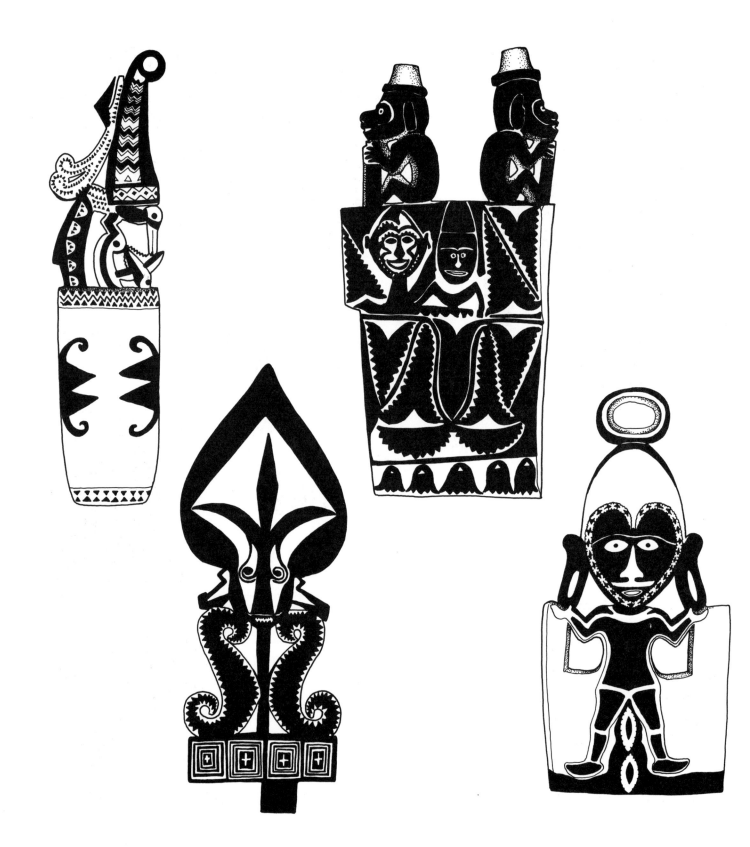

82 Carved and painted wooden canoe ornaments from the Solomon Islands.

83 Carved and painted canoe ornaments from the Solomon Islands, some with shell inlay. The decorations parallel tattoo patterns and ear plugs. TOP RIGHT a seagull fishing float from north-eastern Malaita.

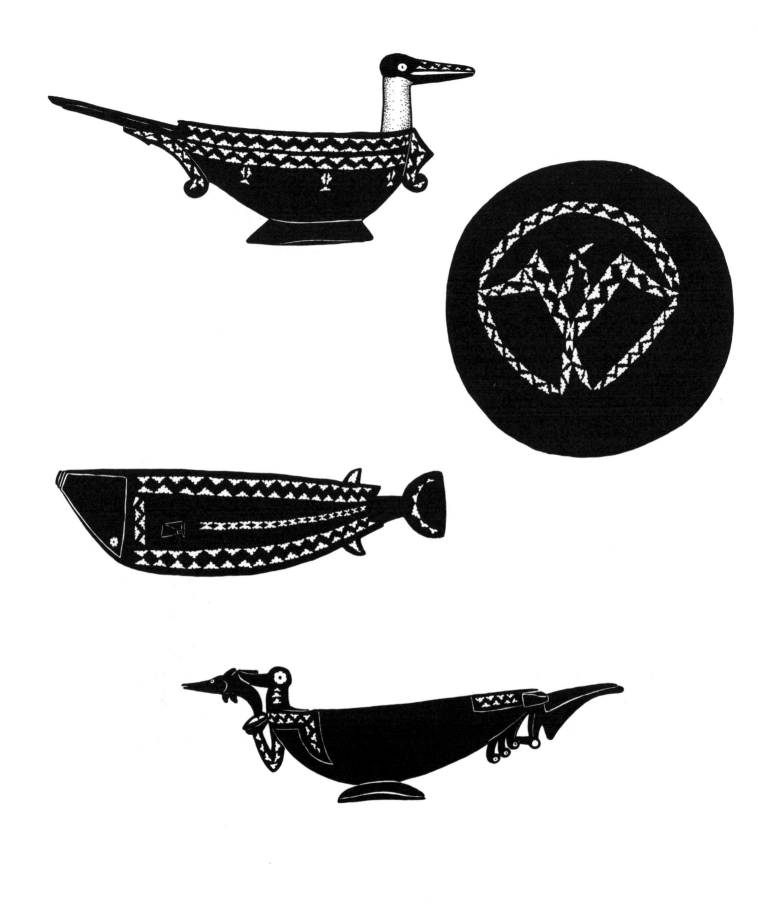

84 Carved wooden food dishes decorated with shell inlay for use at feasts, from the Star Harbour area, eastern Solomon Islands. TOP RIGHT a frigate bird; CENTRE LEFT a box-fish; BOTTOM a bird with a fish in its mouth.

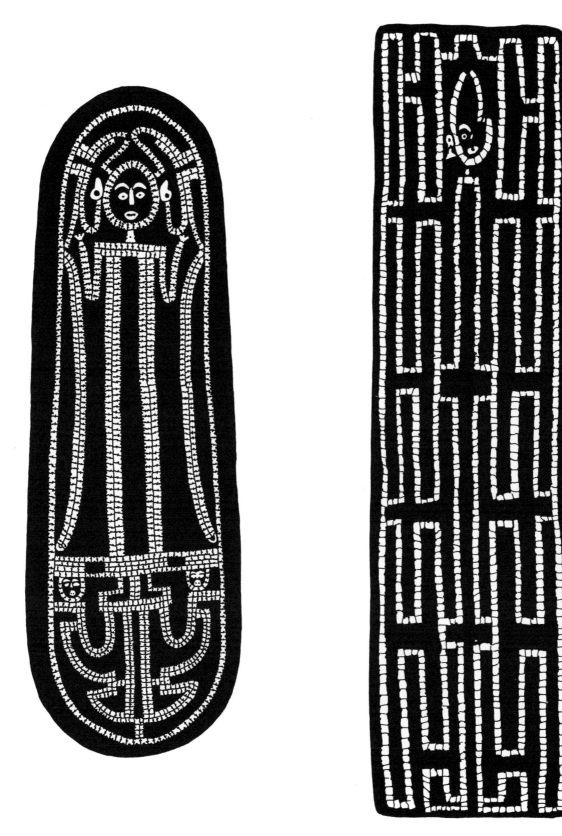

85 Red and black painted shields with shell inlay, made from resin-covered wickerwork, from the Solomon Islands.

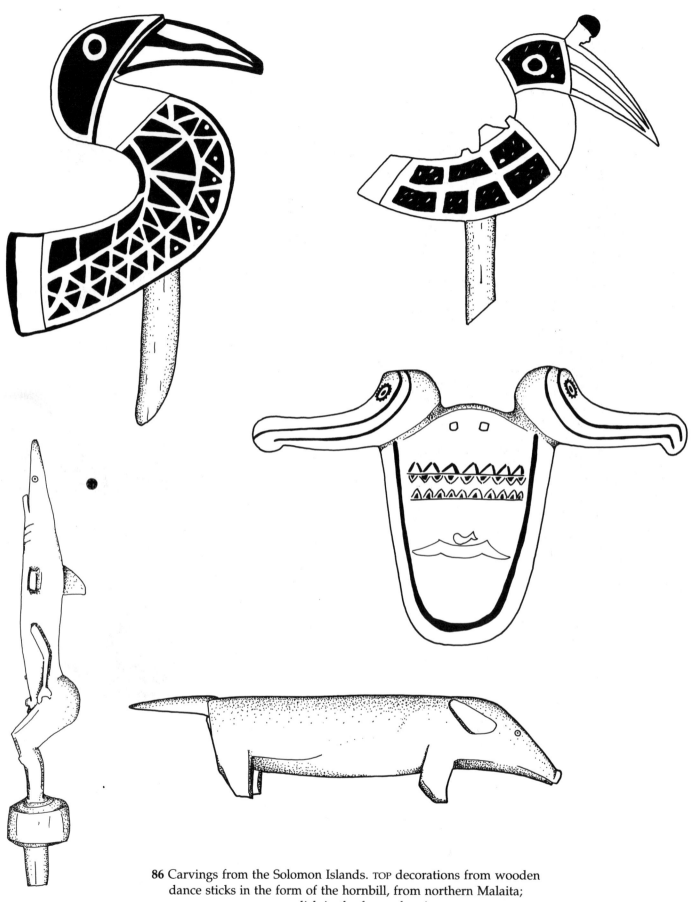

86 Carvings from the Solomon Islands. TOP decorations from wooden dance sticks in the form of the hornbill, from northern Malaita; BOTTOM dish in the form of a pig.

87 LEFT and RIGHT Wooden paddles carved in low relief; CENTRE a dancing club.
The LEFT paddle is carved in the shape of a leaf; LEFT and CENTRE show human figures
wearing head-dresses. All from the Solomon Islands.

88 Carved pendants and nose ornaments in turtle-shell and pearl-shell, from the
Solomon Islands. The designs show frigate birds; TOP LEFT two fish have been
incorporated into the design.

89 Three decorated ceremonial wooden clubs, patterned with incised designs and whitened with lime, from the south-eastern Solomon Islands.

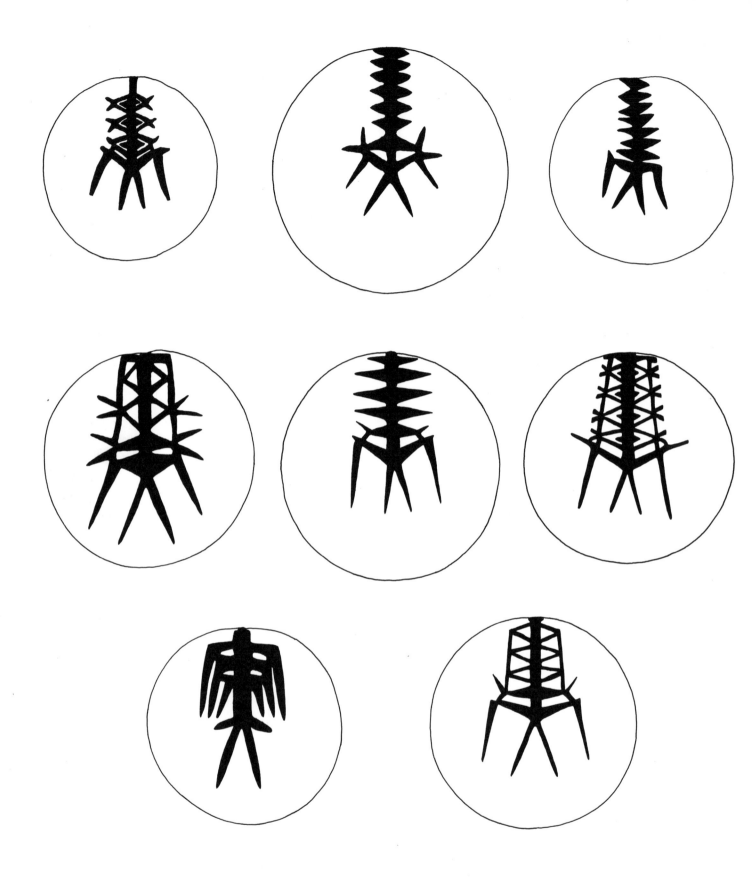

90 *Tema* (neck pendants) from Santa Cruz, Solomon Islands, made from giant clam shells, with turtle-shell overlays carved with an angular motif representing the frigate bird.

91 Painted wooden dance staffs from Santa Cruz, Solomon Islands. The gentle curve of the staffs reflects the curved shape of canoes. They are decorated with geometric designs, some with fish and stylised faces.

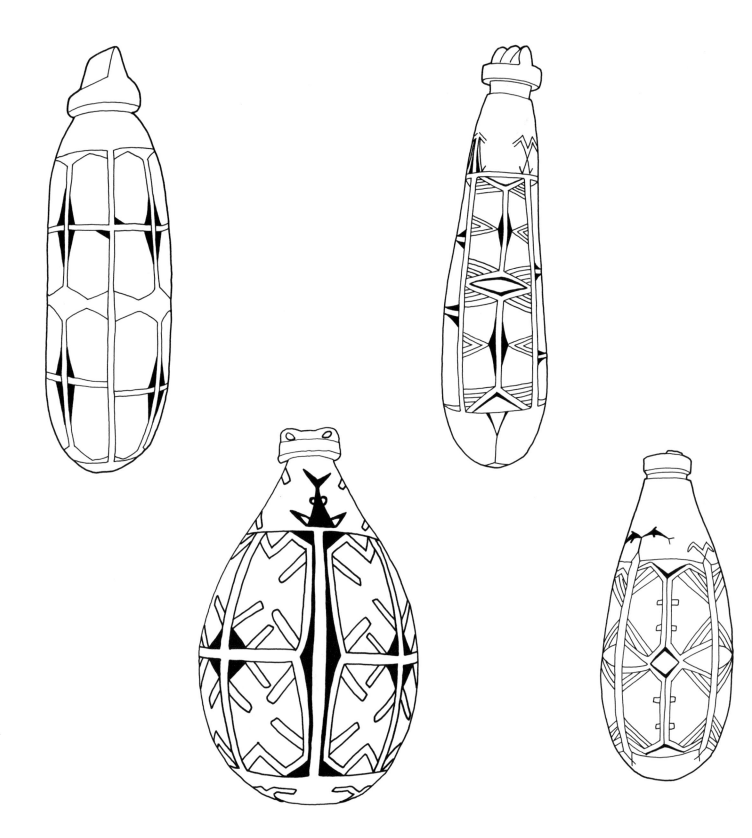

92 Decorated gourd containers with burnt-on geometric designs,
from Santa Cruz, Solomon Islands.

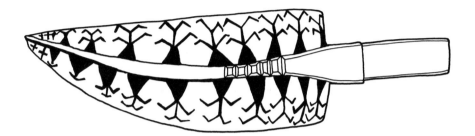

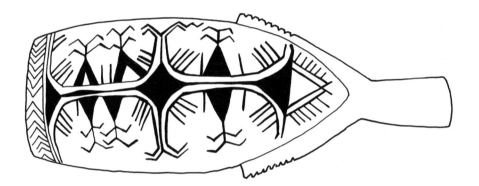

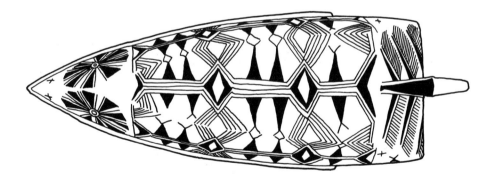

93 Wooden bowls or scoops from Santa Cruz, Solomon Islands, painted with geometric designs. The shape and curves reflect the curve of the island canoes.

94 Woven fibre headbands with stylised figures and faces, from Vanuatu.

97 Decorations including human figures, bats, fish, a palm tree and a boat on two bamboo tubes from New Caledonia.

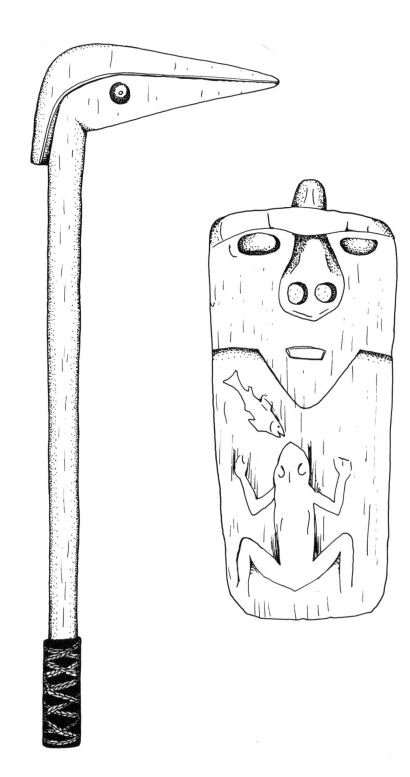

98 Wood carvings from New Caledonia. CENTRE is a wooden club with a stylised bird's head.

99 LEFT and RIGHT Carved wooden house boards; CENTRE a roof finial; all from New Caledonia, where houses were round and thatched.

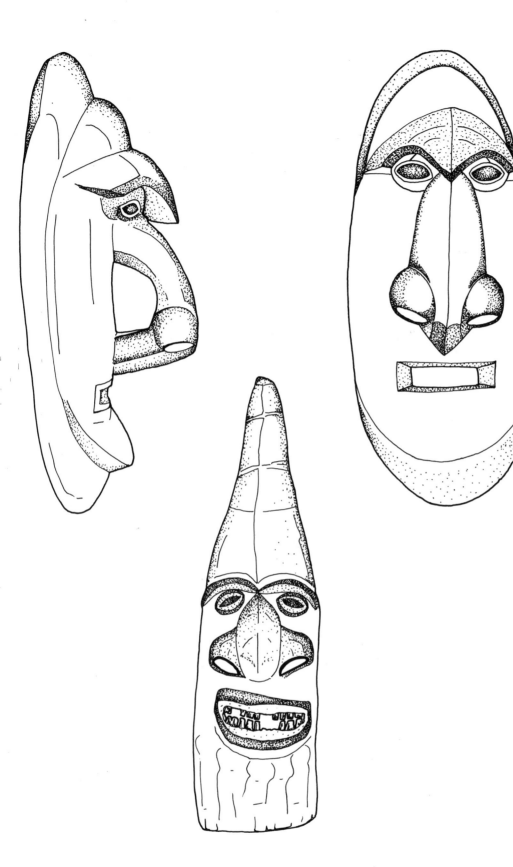

100 Carvings from New Caledonia. The mask TOP LEFT and RIGHT may once have had
attachments of hair and feathers, which was usual for some New Caledonian masks.